Your Brain Is God

Timothy Leary

Ronin

Berkeley, CA

Your Brain Is God

ISBN: 978- 157951- 052- 7
Copyright 1982 by Timothy Leary
Derivative Copyright 2001 by Beverly A. Potter

Published by
RONIN Publishing, Inc.
PO Box 22900
Oakland CA 94609
www. roninpub. com

Manuscript Creation: Beverly Potter
Cover art: Stevee Postman
Cover design: Judy July, Generic Typography

Library of Congress Card Number - 2001118555

This derivative was created by Beverly A. Potter, Ph. D.
from Part Three of *Changing My Mind Among Others*
(1982) by Timothy Leary.

Printed in the United States of America
Distributed by Publishers Group West

Table of Contents

Live Your
Highest Vision.

—Timothy Leary

Introduction

In 1966, the Harvard-Millbrook psychedelic researchers decided to exploit the religious metaphor in order to encourage people to take charge of their own brain functions. I was uneasy about falling back on the religious paradigm. For 40 years I had been conditioned to respond negatively to the word "God." Any time someone started shouting about God, I automatically expected to be conned or threatened by some semiliterate hypocrite.

> I was uneasy about falling back on the religious paradigm.

We tried to avoid this insidious buzzword. God knows, at one point we talked about LSD as a "brain vitamin" or dietary supplement—but this more accurate label sounded dodgy in those days—who knows, perhaps it would fly today in this age of mega-supplements, smart drugs and life-extension. However, self-control of one's diet was not to become respectable until the holistic medicine of the 1970s.

Our own commitments and role-models were always scientific. For example, we succeeded in training illit-

erate prisoners to perform the functions of—and to talk
like—psychologists. And our summer training camps in
the Hotel Catalina in Zihuatenjo, Mexico, effectively taught a wide range of intellectuals how to reimprint
their own brain programs.

Our logic seemed clear—brain-activating drugs ex-
pose people to powerful, mind-blowing experiences that
shatter conventional ideas about reality. If left alone by
society, our International Foundation for Internal Freedom (IFIF) would have succeeded in training several
thousand neurologicians who, in their own communi-
ties, could have trained hundreds of thousands of Americans to use their own heads.

But wisely or foolishly, we got
scared off this scientific approach.
After being expelled from Harvard,
Mexico, Antigua, and Dominica in
the late Spring of 1963, we cravenly
decided that the authorities were
not ready for the 21st Century con-
cept—Every Citizen a Scientist. So we fell back to the
familiar historical turf upon which most earlier freedom
movements had fought the battle—religion.

> Most freedom
> movements
> fought the battle
> on religious turf.

Activating the Divinity Within

Though it might be against the law for responsible
American citizens to use psychoactive plants and drugs
to change their brains, surely 400 years of Western civilization must support the right of Americans to worship
the divinity within, using sacraments that worked for
them. We studied the meaning of the word sacrament,
usually defined as something that relates one to the
divinity. One of the most offensive, flaky characteristics
of 1960s acid-users was their compulsion to babble about
new visions of God, new answers to the Ultimate Secret
of the Universe.

For thousands of years individuals whose brains were activated had chattered about "ultimate secrets" in the context of mystical- personal religious revelation. We were forced to recall that for most of human history, science and philosophy were the province of religion. And most specifically, all references to what we would now call the "psycho- neurological" were described in religious terms.

> Throughout history, individuals with activated brains chattered about "ultimate secrets" in the context of mystical-personal religious revelation.

Our political experiences at Harvard also pushed us in the direction of the religious metaphor. When it became known on campus that a group of psychologists was producing revelatory brain- change, we expected that astronomers and biologists would come flocking around to learn how to use this new tool for expanding awareness. But the scientists, committed to external manipulations, were uninterested. Instead we were flooded by inquiries from the Divinity School.

Brain Change Taboo

Our problem—typical of time- travel agents dealing with primitive cultures—was that a dramatic change in neurology must be gently introduced in the language a culture traditionally uses for those "mysterious, unknown, higher powers" which its science has not yet explained. A review of 20th Century literature showed that there was obviously a strong taboo against "brain- change. " By 1960, indeed, the brain had replaced the genitals as the forbidden organ that must not be touched or turned on by the owner. The only way in which conscious-ness- change experiences could be discussed was in terms of philosophic- religious. Even Buddhism, an atheist method of psychological self- control, allowed itself to be classified as a religion.

Back to the Wisdom of the East

So religion it was. I recall the mo-ment of decision—During a wild, all- night LSD session in our man-sion in the Boston suburbs, Richard Alpert came up to me, eyes popping, and announced, "The East! We must go back to the wisdom of the East! " Go back?

> "The East! We must go back to the wisdom of the East!" Richard Alpert announced.

The lawyers agreed. There is apparently nothing in the Bill of Rights to protect sci-entific freedom. The Constitution was written in a horse- and- buggy pre- technological era. But there was a First Amendment protection of Freedom of Religion.

> There was to be no kneeling down, no dogmas, no holy men, no followers, no churches, no public worship, no financial offerings....

After all, Catholic priests were allowed Communion wine during Prohibition. So I agreed to the religious pos-ture with conditions. There was to be no kneeling down, no dogmas, no holy men, no followers, no churches, no public worship, no financial offerings. . . .

Chapter 1

Do-It-Yourself Theology

Four months after my being fired from Harvard University, the Association of Lutheran Psychologists invited us to make an address at the 1963 American Psychological Association. In the 1950s I had administered psychological screening tests for most of the younger ministers in the Lutheran Church, and so I wondered if my contributions to the faith were, perhaps, being recognized. The address was an attempt to scientize myth and mythologize science. We were trying so romantically to heroicize—sanctify our lives, their lives, life itself.

> I wanted to scientize myth and mythologize science.

The original essay describing my summa theology was widely reprinted in several languages and probably contributed to the blossoming of young visionary scientists who, in the 1980s aged 30 to 45, were pushing out the frontiers of physics, chemistry, and biology. I had been working on the translation of classic issues of theology into the language of modern science for the last 18 years, refining and updating. It was my summa theology and may have been the first compre-

hensive philosophy to deal with evolution, both species
and individual, both past and future.

It is safe to estimate that over a hundred young

I had awakened from a long ontological sleep.

physicists and a like number of
biologists read that first paper at
some point along the way. Imag-
ine yourself an impressionable,
brilliant college student, circa
1964- 70, searching, experiment-
ing, dreaming the dreams of grandeur and idealism and
splendor that characterized that more utopian optimistic
period.

Activist Theology

This is an activist, do- it- yourself theology. God is
defined in terms of the technologies involved in cre-
ating a universe and engineering the obvious stages of
evolution. Anyone interested in playing the God- game
is given suggestions for activating the various levels of
intelligence in hir own brain and DNA and expressing
them through the tools of modern science. Any human
being who wishes to accept the responsibility is offered
the powers traditionally assigned to divinity.

Chapter 2

Sacramental Ritual

 any years ago, on a sunny afternoon in a Cuernavaca garden, I ate seven so-called sacred mushrooms given to me by a scientist from the University of Mexico. During the next five hours, I was whirled through an experience which was, above all and without question, the deepest religious-philosophic experience of my life. And it was totally electric, cellular scientific, cinematographic.

Personal reactions, however passionate, are always relative and may have little general significance. Next come the "Ho Hum" questions, "Why?" and "So what?"

> On a sunny afternoon I ate seven sacred mushrooms and was whirled through an experience that was the deepest religious-philosophic experience of my life.

Many predisposing factors—physiological, emotional, intellectual, ethical-social, financial—cause one person to be ready for a dramatic mind-opening experience and lead another to shrink back from new levels of intelligence. The discovery that the human brain possesses an infinity of potentialities and can operate at

unexpected space- time dimensions left naive me exhila-
rated, awed, and quite convinced that I had awakened
from a long ontological sleep.

Since my brain- activation- illumination of August
1960, 1 have repeated this biochemical and—to me—
sacramental ritual several thousand times, and almost
every subsequent brain- opening has awed me with phil-
osophic- scientific revelations as convincing as the first
experience.

During the 1960- 68 period 1 had been lucky enough
to have collaborated with several hundred scientists and
scholars who joined our various search and research
projects. In our brain- activation centers at Harvard,
in Mexico, Morocco, Almora, India, Millbrook, and
in the California mountains we arranged transcendent
brain- change experiences for several thousand persons
from all walks of life, including more than 400 full- time
religious professionals—about half professing Christian or
Jewish faiths and about half belonging to Celtic, pagan,
or Eastern religions.

Beginnings

In 1962, an informal group of ministers, theologians,
academic hustlers, and religious psychologists in the Harvard environment began meeting once a month to further
these beginnings. This group was the original planning
nucleus of the organizations that assumed sponsorship of
our consciousness- expansion research—IFIF in 1963, the
Castalia Foundation in 1963- 66, and the League for Spiritual Discovery in 1966. That our generating impulse and
original leadership came from a seminar in religious experience may be related to the alarmed confusion we aroused
in secular and psychiatric circles of the time.

The Miracle of Marsh Chapel

The study, sensationalized in the press as "The Miracle of Marsh Chapel, " deserves further elaboration as a "serious . . . controlled" experiment involving over 30 courageous volunteers and as a systematic scientific demonstration of the "religious" aspects of psychedelic experience. This study was the Ph. D. dissertation research of Walter Pahnke, M. D. , then a graduate student in the philosophy of religion at Harvard University, who set out to determine whether the transcendent experience reported during psychedelic acid sessions was similar to the mystical experience reported by saints and religious mystics.

As subjects, 20 divinity students were selected from a group of volunteers and divided into 5 groups of 4 persons. To each group were assigned 2 guides with considerable psychedelic experience—professors and advanced graduate students from Boston- area colleges.

The experiment, believe it or not, took place in a small, private chapel at Boston University, about one hour before noon on Good Friday, 1962. The dean of the chapel, Howard Thurman, was to conduct a public 3- hour devotional service upstairs in the main hall of the church. He visited our subjects a few minutes before the start of the noon service and gave a brief "inspirational" talk.

The experiment, believe it or not, took place in a small, private chapel at Boston University, about one hour before noon on Good Friday, 1962.

Two subjects in each group and one of the two guides were given a moderately stiff dosage of 30 mg. of psilocybin. The remaining two subjects and the second guide received a placebo that produced noticeable somatic side effects such as hot-cold skin flashes, but which was not psychedelic. The study was triple-blind: neither the subjects, guides, nor the experimenters knew who received psilocybin.

We Knew Who Was Who

If you ever run a double-blind study with these drugs, you must not have controls around experimental subjects because no one will be fooled. I knew immediately that two subjects in my group had nicotinic acid; I could tell by their red faces and their restless "game" activity.

> A man walked in, looked out the window, and said, "Magnificent," then turned without looking at us as he walked out. We all knew who was placebo and who was mystical.

But thinking they were on the verge of a mystic experience, they started winking, "Isn't this great? The poor fellows in the other room are being left out of it." Later, after we had been in the chapel and saw other subjects reclining on the floor, obviously completely out of this world, the two called me and said, "Let's go back into the other room." They started playing the drug game again: "How long has it been?" "Gee, I thought I had it." "Now what did you feel exactly?"

A door banged open, and a man walked in, looked out the window, and said, "Magnificent." He turned without looking at us as he walked out. We all knew who was placebo and who was mystical. Typically, 9% of LSD subjects reported unpleasant experiences; most of these fought the experience. In the Good Friday experience, for example, one divinity student fought it all the way, repeating: "Now when is it going to get over? I'm just not in control of myself. Didn't you say it would last four hours?"

There is a magnificent selectivity operating here, because people committed to controlling themselves sense ahead of time that the notion of ego transcendence or loss is threatening. They don't volunteer, don't show up, or postpone it. Of course, courage is the key to creativity or to any relinquishing of ego structure.

> Courage is the key to creativity and to any relinquishing of ego structure.

Expectations

Our studies, naturalistic and experimental, demonstrate that if the expectation, preparation, and setting are Protestant- New England religious, an intense mystical or revelatory experience will be admitted by 40 to 90% of subjects ingesting psychedelic drugs. These results may be attributed to the bias of our research group, which has taken the rather dangerous ACLU position that there are "experiential- spiritual" as well as secular- behavioral emotional- political potentialities of the nervous system.

Five scientific studies by other investigators yield data which indicate that if the setting is supportive but not spiritual, between 40 to 75% of psychedelic subjects will report intense and life- changing philosophic- religious experiences. If the set and setting are supportive and "spiritual," then from 40 to 90% of the experiences will be revelatory and mystico- philosophic- religious.

Philosophic Revelation

How can these results be disregarded by those concerned with philosophic growth and religious development? These data are even more interesting because the experiments took place in 1962, when individual religious

ecstasy—as opposed to religious piety—was highly sus-
pect and when meditation, jogging, yoga, fasting, body
consciousness, social- dropout- withdrawal, and sacramental—organic—foods and drugs were surrounded by
an aura of eccentricity, fear, clandestine secrecy, even
imprisonment.

The 400 professional workers in religious vocations
who partook of psychedelic substances were responsible, thoughtful, and
"moral, " highly moral,
individuals, grimly
aware of the contro-
versial nature of drugs
and aware that their
reputations and jobs
might be undermined.
Not bad, huh? Still the
results read—75% philosophic revelation. It may well be
that, like the finest metal, the most intense religious experience requires fire, the "heat" of police constabulatory
opposition, to produce the keenest edge. When sacramental biochemicals are used as routinely and tamely as
organ music and incense the ego- shattering, awe- inspiring effect of the drugs may be diminished.

> How can these results
> be disregarded by those
> concerned with philosophic
> growth and religious
> development?

> Like the finest metal, the most intense
> religious experience requires fire, the "heat"
> of police constabulatory opposition, to
> produce the keenest edge.

Chapter 3

Eight Crafts
of God

The religious experience is the ecstatic, jolt-
ing, wondrous, awe-struck, life-changing,
mind-boggling confrontation with one or all of
the eight basic mysteries of existence. The goal of an
intelligent life, according to Socrates, is to pursue the
philosophic quest—to increase one's knowledge of self
and world. Now there is an important division of labor
involved in the philosoph-
ic search. Religion, being
personal and private, cannot produce answers to the
eight basic questions.

> It is science that
> produces the
> ever-changing, improving
> answers to the haunting
> questions that religious
> wonder poses.

The philosopher's role is
to ignite the wonder, raise
the burning issues, inspire
the pursuit of answers. It
is science that produces the ever-changing, improving
answers to the haunting questions that religious wonder
poses. There are eight questions which any fair survey of
our philosophic history would agree are most fundamen-
tal to our existential condition.

Eight Fundamental Questions

Category	Type of Questions	Examples
Origins	Genesis	How, when, where did life come from? How has it evolved?
Politics	Security	Why do humans fight and compete destructively? What are the territorial laws that explain conflict? How can humans live in relative peace and harmony? How, when, where, and why do humans differ (among each other and from other mammalian species) in aggression, control, cooperation, affiliation?
Epistem-ology	Truth, fact, knowledge, language, communications, manufacture of objects, artifacts, & symbol systems	How, when, where, and why does the mind emerge (in the individual and species)? And how, when, where, and why do humans differ in their ability to process information, learn, communicate, think, plan, and manufacture?
Ethics	Good and evil, right and wrong.	How, when, where, and why do humans differ in their moral beliefs and rituals? Who decides what is good and right?
Esthetics	Beauty, pleasure luxury, sensory reward.	How, when, where, and why do humans devote their energies to decration, hedonism, art, music, entertainment? And how, where, when, and why do they differ in modes of pleasure?

Ontology	Reality and its (their) definition.	How, when, where, and why do humans differ in the realities they construct and inhabit? How are realities formed and changed?
Teleology	Evolution & de-evolution of life.	What are the stages and mechanisms of evolution? Where, when, how, and why has evolution occurred? Chance? Natural selection? Natural election? Creation? If life is created and evolution blueprinted, who did it? Where is life going?
Cosmology	Galactic evolution, of ultimate and basic structure.	How, when, where, and why was matter-energy formed? What are the basic units and patterns of matter/energy? What are the basic forces, energies, and plans that hold the universe together (or don't) and determine its evolution? Where are we going?

The Navigational Question

Now it is true that most human beings spend little time thinking about these issues. Mundane questions about how to get fed, how to avoid irritable neighbors, which career to follow, which girl to marry, who will win the Super Bowl obsess the normal consciousness of most humans.

The religious- philosophic person is defined by hir concern for the great navigational question. The answers, we recall, come from the listening posts which we set up to obtain from nature the signals which will increase our knowledge about what nature is up to.

Scientific Answers

The 19th Century was one of considerable religious disarray and confusion. On the one hand, the old creeds have obviously not succeeded in producing survivally- safe answers. When the Catholic church threatens eternal damnation for believers who do not follow St. Paul's 1st Century taboos against birth control—at a time when starvation and overpopulation are endemic in Catholic countries—a certain nervousness develops. When the 1,000- year- old warfare between Christianity and Islam erupts again in the 87th crusade—Rockefeller vs Khomeini- Khadafi—again, sensible people wonder what these aging religious fundamentalists really have in mind for the future of our species.

Now our species can answer the basic questions as well as take over the technologies for running the universe.

Suddenly there is an explosion of new scientific insights—nuclear physics, astrophysics, genetics, neurology, ethology—which produce data requiring drastic changes

in our conceptions of human nature. We face the splen-
did, glorious, possibility that, now, for the first time,
the planet was the genetic future. It is surely time for a
global celebration! Finally our species is on the thresh-
old of living, not in helpless fear and ignorance, but in
confident loving hope!

Scientific Paganism

As we survey these new findings which allow us to
learn and practice the eight technologies of God, we
are delighted to discover that certain ancient religions,
mainly the pagan, in millennia past had anticipated what
our scientists are now discovering. And as Americans
we are proud to point out that
the 1960s drug- culture's gid-
dy, wild, confused eruption of
philosophy and spiritual anar-
chy played an important role in
stimulating and provoking the
new Scientific Paganism of the
21st Century. The new scientific answers provide us with
eight new definitions of God as
designer/ technologist of the universe. And they suggest
how any serious- minded intelligent person can begin to
master these Eight Crafts of Divinity.

> The new scientific
> answers provide
> us with eight new
> definitions of
> God as designer/
> technologist of
> the universe.

Chapter 4

Origins

Our fundamentalist Judeo-Christian friends assure us that life was created by a stern, omnipotent, judgmental condominium-owner named Jehovah and that our destinies follow Hir impenetrable plans.

Most religions throughout history have offered metaphorical or poetic myths which, unfortunately, developed in prescientific days before Copernicus, Darwin or Galileo. Giordano Bruno was not the only one to be killed for suggesting that the universe is a big, wild, place filled with other centers of intelligence.

> *God #1 is the Single-cell Intelligence, the collaborative brain that knows how to run a simple protozoan. The First God is the one-celled God. The first and original craft of God is Protozoan.*

During the past fifty years, astronomy, exo-biology, and genetics have produced wondrous scenarios of Big Bangs, Black Holes, alternate universes, accidental or directed panspermia—seeding of planets from space, and the ultimate cosmic unifying principle, that every atom in our bodies has come from the supernova explosions of far-distant stars.

For us, as a species momentarily stranded in a land-locked terrestrial stage, life began locally in the ocean, in unicellular form. We clumsy, heavy bipeds, clinging like barnacles on the grasping 1-G surface of an embryonic planet tend to overestimate our status and function in the evolutionary web.

Everything that we now possess as physiological or neural equipment was built into the original design of the first protozoan cells.

The unicellular state is the first, the most basic, the omnipresent triumphant form of intelligent life. Everything that we now possess as physiological or neural equipment was built into the original design of the first protozoan cells.

We Began as a Single Cell

Individually, too, we began as a single cell at the moment of our conception. Only recently have we begun to understand the seed-complexity of our beginnings. The single cell handles more transactions per day than do the nine million primates of New York City.

As we decipher the tactics and intelligent operations of the single cell, we shall begin to understand how our own lives can be better arranged. This is especially obvious when we consider that our original germ cell contained the blueprints for designing the equipment which makes it possible for us to write, edit, print, distribute, buy and read this book.

God the Protozoan

Mystics and psychedelic drug users have commented
eloquently on the unicellular pageantry and wisdom that
accompanies transcendent moments. Much of vision-
ary- drug art is protozoan- from Bosch to Sufi rugs to
acid- rock light shows. Our LSD subjects regularly report
accessing those large circuits of our brain that are tuned
into cellular traffic.

   At the most down- to- earth level, we cannot move
into outer space until we realize that life- on- earth is a
giant unified cellular entity.
The Gaia Theory, which
we shall consider at later
stages of theotechnology,
reminds us that the space
capsules in which we will

> Unicellular pageantry
> and wisdom accompanies
> transcendent moments.

escape from this planet will inevitably be based on unicellular design. Is it not clear that the launch- out from
the planet will require us to fabricate self- sustaining
capsules that must be capable of performing the most
rudimentary unicellular behaviors?

Chapter 5

Predator-Prey Politics

ost religions play on home- territory senti-
ments and seek to establish political- mili-
tary- police- predator control. Position in the
pecking order had always been influenced, if not determined, by religious status. Until 1960, for example,
only a predator Protestant could become president of the
United States.

> *God #2 is the presocial, wily-animal god of emo-
> tion-locomotion that resides within our nervous
> system, ready to pour out flight-fight endocrine
> juices. The Second Craft of God is intelligent
> access to and control of emotions.*

Religions activate midbrain centers that mediate mammalian, emotional territorial behavior. Dumb religions
stimulate defense of home turf aggression- control and
submission docility. The smarter religions stimulate migration. Judeo- Christian- Moslem, Marxist religions glorify
conquest, expansion, and murder of nonbelievers. The
deliberate incitement of chauvinist- partisan fear- and- rage
is a standard tactic in most human theologies.

Anthropocentric Philosophies

Ethology and sociobiology observe the behavior of animals in natural habitats and study the reflex methods of social organization used by other species—territoriality, caste division of labor, bluff, slavery, gestural communication, olfactory signaling, migration, hierarchy. There seems to be no social problem discussed in the Judeo-Christian Bible that has not been solved more harmoniously and intelligently by social insects.

> The deliberate incitement of chauvinist-partisan fear-and-rage is a standard tactic in most human theologies.

Eastern religions—non-urban and thus more in tune with nature—have developed ecological sensitivities that are in agreement with the recent insights of sociobiologists. Surely it is time for grim, suspicious, fear-rage mammalian Islamo-Christian sects to adopt a more genial, tolerant perspective of interspecies or intraspecies collaboration.

The psychedelic drug experimentation of the 1960s produced one wonderful bi-product—a pagan love of nature, a hippy sense of alienation from man-made anthropocentric philosophies. Is it not clear that the ecology movement owes its birth to barefoot acid-pagan concern for nature?

Here again, we see that brains activated by psychedelic drugs readily accept the findings of modern science, restate the Oriental life-affirming philosophies of Buddhism, Jainism, Hinduism and make possible the Scientific Paganism of the 21st Century.

That's Dangerous, Man!

When I was studying mammalian theology at Folsom prison in 1973, it was my custom, during the clear, blue-sky, desert-hot summer months, to walk barefoot in the prison yard. One day the leader of the Hell's Angels, his name was James "Fu" Griffin, approached me.

"Hey, man," he said, "how come you walk barefoot in the prison yard? Don't you know that's dangerous?" We were the best of friends and his question was solicitous, not hostile. He wanted nothing but the best for me.

"Why is it dangerous?" I asked.

"Well you're exposed. Like to germs and all. You know all these animals spit on the ground here."

"Yeah, I know. But here's how I look at it. When you walk barefoot, like undefended, you are very alert about where you put your feet. I'm more alive, like a wild animal, when I'm barefoot. And, come to think of it, I believe it would be better if more prisoners here stopped spitting on the yard and joined me walking barefoot."

"I see what you mean," said James "Fu" Griffin.

He subsequently got a degree in anthropology from Berkeley and later became a country-Western promoter in San Francisco.

Loco-Motions

Psychopharmacology, particularly in its use of the tranquilizers, has introduced the notion of "turning off" irrelevant or inappropriate emotion, thus giving medical respectability to the Hindu and hipster notion of being "cool." Let us consider a dictionary definition. "Emotion: agitation of the passions or sensibilities often involving physiological changes. Rage, fear, greed, desire, gratitude, jealousy, self-pity. " Is this any way to run a species? Why do these loco-motions play such a visible part in human life?

Mediterranean

Personal emotions are poetically considered to be a diagnostic symptom of humanity. Mr. Spock, of *Star Trek* is "alien" because he does not break down in irrational outbursts, fits of temper, or sentiment. If now and then a tiny little tear of self-pity would appear in Spock's eye we would consider him one-of-us. To be human is, for many psychologists, to be honestly irrational. One shows one's "real nature" when some unpleasant feeling is revealed.

This romantic view of human nature is clearly Mediterranean. Now that our species is ready to send advanced probes into space it is a matter of amusement that our species-identity is influenced by a bunch of semi-illiterate Bronze-Age Greeks, Italians, and Semites. Saint Augustine was a fanatic, superstitious Libyan. Aristotle was an Athenian living in a barbarous era when treachery, ignorance, fanaticism were endemic. Old Testament drama, vulgarized by Italian opera and homogenized in our modern prime-time soap opera, has insidiously glorified emotions—mammalian, male-macho meanness, and self-pity. Even today this humorless, jumpy fanaticism arises from the Mediterranean basin like an adrenaline smog.

> Emotional actions are the most contracted, dangerous form of fanatic stupor. Emotions are addictive, narcotic, and stupefacient.

God the Emotional Mammal

Romantic poetry and fiction of the last 2, 000 years has quite blinded us to the fact that emotions are a low mammalian form of jungle consciousness. Emotional actions are the most contracted, dangerous form of fanatic stupor. Any peasant, any child can tell you that. Beware of emotions. Watch out for the emotional person, the heavy-breathing lurching Latin lunatic. The emotional person is turned off sensually. Hir body is a churning robot; s/he has lost all connection with cellular wisdom or atomic revelation. Emotions are addictive, narcotic, and stupefacient. Like an alcoholic or a junkie, the frightened person activates hir favorite mammalian circuit.

Moods such as sorrow and joy accompany emotions. Like a junkie who has just connected, the emotional person feels good when s/he has scored emotionally—i. e, put someone down or been beaten down.

Conscious love is not an emotion; it is serene merging with yourself, with other people, with other forms of energy. Love cannot exist in an emotional state. The great kick of the mystic experience is the sudden relief from emotional pressure. The only state in which we can learn, harmonize, grow, merge, join, understand, is the absence of emotion called security, attained through fine-tuning the emotions.

> The great kick of the mystic experience is the sudden relief from emotional pressure.

Emergency Alarms

Why, then, if emotions are so painful, demanding, and blinding, are they built into the human repertoire for a basic survival purpose? Emotions are emergency alarms.

The organism at the point- of- death threat or territorial invasion goes into a paroxysm of frantic activity, like a fish out of water, like a cornered animal.

The sensible animal avoids situations that elicit fear. Your wise animal prefers to lay back relaxed- using his senses, tuned into his delicious body- organ music, closing his eyes to drift back in cellular memory. Dogs and cats are high—alertly cool, all the time—except when bad luck demands emotional measures.

Evolution works through recapitulation, adding new somaticneural circuits to the old, requiring each individual to repeat the evolutionary stages of the species. Each of us has a mammalian midbrain geared for territorial security, physical safety, offensive. In order to perform any of the "higher" functions of intelligence, we must satisfy the midbrain. We must arrange our lives so that we feel "at home," cozy, safe in a territorial niche, with adequate food supply.

It is also part of survival wisdom to check out, dry- run, our animal emotional repertoire. Flick through the paranoia dials regularly. What would I do if an armed robber stole into the house at midnight? What would I do if jumped by some hoods in the parking lot? What would I do if the underclasses break out of the ghetto or the rednecks invade the ghetto?

Like all our divinities, the presocial, wily- animal god of emotion- locomotion resides within our nervous system, ready to pour out flight- fight endocrine juices. Politicians and priests deliberately play on our fears and exaggerate our dangers for their own profit. This is the National Security ploy. The intelligent human being has learned to turn- on- and- off the emotions, the way you navigate the other circuits in your brain.

Chapter 6

Epistemology

How do we know? Why do we think and believe what we think and believe? How do we determine what is true and what is fact? Why will people believe even the most bizarre notions? Why do people, especially establishment priests and scientists, deliberately refuse to learn lessons basic to survival and happiness? How come people believe fanatically in such different and opposing ways? Why are brains equipped or programmed or conditioned to perform such different functions? Why do minds work the way they do?

> *God #3 is the semanticist. In the beginning was the Word. S/He who creates new words and new grammars becomes the Divinity of Thought. The Third Craft of God is semantics.*

That these questions still remain unanswered after 3,000 years of Eastern-Western philosophy reflects the primitive, primate nature of our species. Many religions include an epistemological theory of truth-fact. Most assert that truth was revealed once and for all by an inaccessible Deity in the form of Sacred Writings. And most religions nominate priesthoods—a lawyer-scribe caste—who arbitrate, interpret, and enforce—with violence—the Divine Truths revealed in the Bibles, Korans, Torahs in cultures where truth-fact are tied to religious dogmas, then science wanes, practical investigation languishes, and thinking is subordinated to submissive belief.

But once again, we see that some Eastern religions, Zen, for example, and some Western philosophies— particularly the semantic—have understood the crucial difference between the map and the territory, between the avalanche of raw data processed by the brain and the pitifully few abstractions which we use to label reality. More recently, linguists and cognitive psychologists and ethologists have produced data that help us understand how the cognitive function emerges in species and in individual humans.

Evolutionary Intelligence

Around the age of 6 in the individual human—and around 25 million years ago in the age of our species— the Evolutionary Intelligence arranges to activate frontal lobes. Only when our primate ancestors had learned to walk on two feet, thus freeing their mouths for oral signaling, could the new laryngeal-manual circuits of the brain emerge.

A key factor in the evolution of intelligence is socialization

Obviously people are born with different brains. A key factor in the evolution of intelligence is socialization. Division of labor. Gaia works with gene pools, which produce specialized castes, individuals genetically geared to perform the different functions that contribute variously to the needs of the group. Sociobiologists have ruminated obsessively to explain altruism in social animals. Why does one bird give the alarm signal when the hawk is sighted? This seems to violate the "selfish gene" principle of natural selection. By drawing attention to himself, the flock "crier" risks his own reproductive future.

One possible answer—that of inborn caste difference—has so far eluded the ethologists. Some birds are caste- equipped with nervous systems geared to scan more restlessly, and to react with speedier alarm- signalry. Other birds in the flock are equipped with nervous systems caste- calibrated for more accurate homing, food selection, or for just plain old dull following, thus adding population mass, in swarming numbers, to the gene pool. Surely commonsense observation of human heredity shows us that genius brains can emerge from the dullest normal of the kith- kin.

Brain Castes

A human group requires a variety of brain castes to perform the highly specialized and complex acts necessary to keep the collective unit going. People are born with different minds, equipped with brains designed to be better at certain mental functions. Our minds are "made up" for us at the moment of conception. Twentieth Century mass education methods disastrously assumed that equal Ivy League education for all was the neurological goal of a democratic or even a socialist society.

> A human group requires a variety of brain castes.

Mass education has not worked. Millions of Johnnies now find themselves in college, still unable to read, because a majority of brains today are not designed to process abstract symbols rapidly, pleasurably, obsessive-

ly. Probably not more than 10% of Americans' brains
are geared to comfortably handle symbols, that is, to
read and write. Most legally literate people read only
when necessary, and then with discomfort. Many highly
successful nonreaders have learned in parrot fashion to
recognize and rote- repeat symbol combinations. But
they are incapable of producing personal original verbal communication. Writing ability cannot be taught.
Those who are called "writers" or "literary" may make
up a special small caste, necessary to provide specified
functions in the social hive. My God, if everyone were
a "literary writer" no one would be left to manage the
store.

Thinking Fixed Early

So genetics and sociobiology give us one basic answer to
the question: How are our minds made up? The sec-
ondary answer to the epistemology question is linguis-
tic- neurological. Each child—and gene pool—is perma-
nently "fixed" in a mental- linguistic style of thinking,
during the critical period when the linguistic circuits of
the brain are being activated. The 6 1/ 2- year- old imprints the sign- systems and signal attitudes that happen
to impinge on his nervous system. The mental complexity level of the home, neighborhood, and cultural
Zeitgeist determines the texture of one' s mentation.

Many a Newton and Einstein has lived and died
in dumb cultures that could not provide the vulnera-
ble brain with the level of symbol complexity required.
Teachers—a critical aspect of the "mental environment"—are, of course, themselves members of a mental caste, crucial genetic agents designed to perpetuate
unquestioningly the hive culture. Their function is to
instill, in rote manner, the symbols and thinking- modes
of the society. They succeed with that large majority of

students, themselves bred for unthinking hive performance.

But teachers often run into problems with young members of the "thinking" caste, neurally geared to invent, originate abstractions. It is sufficient only that this caste be exposed to the current symbol techniques. They are geared to really understand symbols so that they can improve them.

An American teacher is faced with the problem of transmitting symbol manipulation methods to at least 8 brain-models, each geared to think in a way very different from the others. The confusion among these specialized castes, each of which operates under the illusion that it is the "smartest", is the history of philosophy.

> Teachers must transmit symbol manipulation methods to at least 8 brain-models each geared to think in a different way.

It is the great semantic revelation of Sapir, Whorf, Chomsky, Korzybski, Wittgenstein, that symbols define a special reality-level of their own, separate from the realities they naively assume to represent. In the beginning was the Word. This defines God the Semanticist.

Chapter 7

Ethics

One of the principal functions of pre-scientific religions was the definition of social-domestic-sexual roles and legislation of the moral codes that guided approved interactions among the various roles. Thou shalt not covet thy neighbor's wife and other chattel goods. Thou shalt not covet thy neighbor's car. Herd acceptability, social conformity are survival necessities in civilizations controlled by religious orthodoxy.

> God #4 is the moralist. The Fourth God
> is accepting responsibility and moving beyond
> hive-docility. The Fourth Craft of God is the
> fabrication of your own new morality—freer,
> more intelligent and more genetically evolved.

Domestication of consciousness by the monolithic state is an inevitable stage in species and individual evolution. Although most of humanity despises its rulers, it is impossible to change the cultural-moral structure of a society. The recent return to fundamentalism in Iran and other Moslem countries indicates how geography determines social behavior.

Drop Out

For millennia, Oriental religions have taught that a
"drop-out" from conventional roles was necessary for
personal growth, but this detachment from hive moral-
ity has been difficult in highly organized western states.
The recent establishment of global
communication nets, particularly movies, television, transistor
radios, has presented humans
with alternate lifestyles and moral
codes. The peasant in Ceylon,
the office worker in Budapest learn
what cultural modes are acceptable in other lands. This leads to
migration. And migration typically leads to changes in
religion and social roles.

> Oriental religions have long encouraged dropping out for personal growth.

God the moralist is a watchful, jealous divinity.
Priests and moral commissars typically do everything
possible to maintain cultural conformity and to prevent
migration. More than two-thirds of the United Nations
demand exit visas to prevent citizens leaving to seek
another lifestyle.

Seek Within

The psychedelic revolution of the late 20th Century encouraged millions of people to seek within to find
navigational coordinates for the voyage of life. It was
to be expected that a mass "turn on" would lead to a
widespread "drop-out" phenomenon. The typical LSD
bad-trip panic occurred when the subject discovered the
rubber-stamp artificial nature of social reality and social
role; realized that one's identity is a fragile role in a flimsy historical vaudeville show.

This freedom is wrong! Get me back to my safe cubicle in the urban hive! If I am not my social role, who am I? What will the neighbors and the moralists think? If I violate the taboos defining my cultural identity, I will offend God.

If you want to move beyond hive-docility you must become God, the Moralist.

The solution is, of course, to accept the responsibility. Each person who wishes to move beyond hive- docility must become God the Moralist just as the old Hindus said.

Chapter 8

Esthetics

ost post-pagan, organized, civilized religions have been inspired by God the Moralist Dictator, who invariably proscribed, under the pain of eternal punishment, the pleasures of sensuality, eroticism, individual—as opposed to priesthood—luxury and free art. These taboos are comprehensible because a citizenry that pursues pleasure will tend to pay less attention to domestication roles and the self-sacrifices that benefit society.

> God #5 is the hedonic artist. The Fifth God is the esthetic director of the sensory world that one constructs and blissfully inhabits. The Fifth Craft of God is management of one's own body.

Centralized monotheisms understandably denounced paganism. The looseness of the nature worshipper had to be tightened up to maintain an urban, post-tribal society. The Eastern and Mideastern empires reserved luxury, art, sensuality to the aristocracy.

God the Hedonic Artist

The concept of God the Hedonist emerged in Greece in the centuries before Christ. Here the wonderful notions of individuality and democracy first blossomed. If the singular human being is the unit of life, then naturally the individual is going to develop a personal philosophy and select hir own style of self-reward. The idea of beauty, the adoration of the human body, its grooming, nurture, play, display, and its harmony with esthetic environments has lasted through the hegemonies of Alexander, Rome, Catholicism, flared up magnificently in the Renaissance, rode the wave of Protestantism, and appeared in the 20th Century in the form of the Bohemian, the artist, the entertainer, the designer, the playboy-playglrl.

> Some religions have fitfully allowed cults that focus on somatic energy and sacred sensuality.

Some religions have fitfully allowed cults that focus on somatic energy and sacred sensuality. Tantra—both Bengali and Tibetan, Zen, Hasidic Judaism preserved the notions of kundalini, chakra consciousness, spiritual-eroticism, ecstatic exuberance, mystic altered states. But Hedonism has always been easily checked by centralized religious states and restricted to a specialized caste of artists usually patronized and tolerated by the rulers. This worked out well. The masters needed the hedonic estheticians to entertain and beautify while the great mass of the citizenry was kept in submissive asceticism. The lowest classes and the outside minorities were usually allowed to indulge themselves in gross sensuality, sternly condemned by bourgeois moralists.

In the 20th Century, the concept of selfhood suddenly became popularized and vulgarized. Two world wars
moved people around, lessening the hold of parochial
moral censors. Psychoanalysis introduced the notion of
self-improvement. The explosion of the film/video culture trained the citizenry to dial and tune the entertain-
ment they wished. The material consumerism mania of
the 1950's strengthened the idea that the working person
was entitled to choose what looked good—purchasable
things, that is.

Resurrection of the Body

In the 1960's, the 2,500-year-old tradition of self-discov-
ery and self-indulgence finally blossomed as a mass phenomenon. The widespread use of
hedonic drugs led to a resurrection
of the body. Sensual consumerism.
Sexual liberation. Erotic dress,
dance, talk, print, film, music.
Wholistic health methods. Diet,
jogging, trendy style. The working
person discovered that hir own body
belonged, not to the state or to
the moralist or to the authoritarian
doctor, but to hirself.

> One of the
> ecstatic
> horrors of the
> LSD experience
> is the sudden
> confrontation
> with your
> own body.

The continually expanding use of brain-activating
drugs in the 1970's built up the hedonic momentum
because of the obvious neurological fact that drugs turn
on the body. One of the ecstatic horrors of the LSD
experience is the sudden confrontation with your own
body. You are catapulted into the matrix of quadrillions
of squirming cells and somatic communication systems,
swept down the tunnels and canals of your own wa-
terworks. You have visions of microscopic processes,
strange, undulating tissue patterns. You are pummeled

down the fantastic artistry of internal factories, recoiling with fear or shrieking in pleasure at the incessant push, struggle, drive of the biological machinery at every moment engulfing you.

Heaven Within

Here is the ancient wisdom of gnostics, hermetics, Sufis, Tantric gurus, yogis, occult healers. Your body is the mirror of the macrocosm, the kingdom of heaven within you. Tibetan and Indian tantras and modern psychology workshops train the student to pay attention to the body's energies and messages.

> Your body is the mirror of the macrocosm, the kingdom of heaven within you.

By 1981 the intelligent American was beginning to define hir body as a complex receiving station, a sacred communications satellite, a bipedal telescope, a mosaic of touching, sniffing, listening, tasting microphones picking up vibrations from planetary energy systems, a worldwide retinal ABC, an eardrum RCA, an International Smell and Tell, a consolidated General Foods laboratory. God of un-common sense.

Chapter 9

Ontology

Every religion has, explicitly or implicitly, tried to answer the question: What is reality? Most theologies have held that reality is defined by the dogmas and rules of the priesthood. Certain great Oriental philosophers and some mystic Western sages have understood that reality is a unified, complex, myriad maya play of all energies, which cluster and organize into transient structures called matter. And that what one believes to be real simply reflects the relativistic perspective of the beholder.

> *God #6 is the neurologician. The Sixth God is the neurological engineer, the reprintable brain that rebuilds neural realities. The Sixth God is the neurologician. The Sixth Craft of God is psychopharmacology to dial and tune one's own brain.*

These prescientific intimations of ontological relativity remained mystical until the neurological and pharmacological advances of the 20th Century. The brain, for so long a taboo organ, shrouded in mystery, was now recognized as the seat of consciousness, the tool for fabricating reality. We realize that everything we experience is computed by the brain; that we can go outward into the universe or inward to study the nucleus of the atom only as far and precisely as our neuro- receptive, neuro- associative, and neuro- transmission intelligence allows us.

God the Neurologician

As long as we rely on our brains to know, then inevitably we shall define the universe as an enormous brain. Each flick of energy, stellar- galactic or nuclear- atomic, is seen as information. The universe is a web of intelligence mediated by our brain. The smarter we become, the more intelligent the universe will become. The more skillful we become in managing our own brains—our reality tools, the more skillful we shall become in fabricating, managing universes. The smarter we become, the smarter God will become.

> The smarter we become the smarter God becomes.

Recent scientific discoveries have indicated how imprinting creates the chessboard of our realities and how conditioning keeps the social, intellectual, emotional, and survival games going. The suggestion that humans can systematically reimprint, rebuild their realities has, for the first time in human history, raised the intelligence of our species to the level of self- mastery and self- control, by the individual, of hir own neural realities.

Chapter 10

Evolution

Theories of evolution or devolution are built into almost every religion. Hinduism teaches that life spins in long cycles or ages—kalpas—winding down from the most harmonious to the apocalyptic end, and then begins all over again. This, like most Oriental philosophies, is a pessimistic, quietist, makes-no-difference doctrine of devolution. Why bother? Everything is terrible and the future is going to get worse. The only thing to do is cool out and try to get off the wheel of existence.

> *God #7 is the geneticist-sociobiologist. The Seventh God, the Geneticist, accomplishing the routine tasks of divinity-create life, improve life, attain immortality. The Seventh Craft of God is management of DNA.*

God the Geneticist-Sociobiologist

Western monotheisms have generally denied the theory of evolution. A jealous God built the universe and created mankind, and the stages to come depend on how

obedient you are to His priests. There is no sense of how
we have evolved and certainly no specific notion that we
are still evolving into a better future. Indeed, the concept of a future which could be predicted or constructed
is of very recent origin.

According to biologists, the flame of life that moves
every living form, including the cell cluster you call
your self, was seeded as a tiny single-celled spark in
the lower Precambrian mud, then unfolded in steady,
preprogrammed transformations to more complex forms.
But the single cell's still thriving, thank you. Next,
your ancestral fire glowed in seaweed, algae, flagellate,
sponge, coral—about 1 billion years ago; then scorpion,
millipede, fish—about 600 million years ago.

Every cell in your body traces back—about 450 million years—to the same light life flickering in our amphibian ancestors—and what a risky mutation migration
to leave the sea! From the shoreline, the mastery of terrestrial environment accel-
erated into four-foot mammalian intelligence—stronger, fiercer, faster. Then
the great moment when we
stood erect freeing throat
and hands for signalling and
manipulation—and started climbing trees. Higher has
always been the trajectory of intelligent evolution. From
the trees we developed gesture and rudimentary language. Watch out for that lion! Piss on that tiger!

Higher has always been
the trajectory of
intelligence evolution.

Then the development of a tool-culture, agriculture,
trade, cities organizing enormous insectoid cultures. And
more recently, now, the development of that greatest tool
of evolution—The Self, mastering the body, the brain,
and now DNA—the code of evolution itself.

Recapitulating the Cycle

Most wonderfully, each of us has recapitulated this sequence of evolution in our own personal lives. We were
single-celled creatures when we were conceived and
we retraced in our mothers' wombs, the same genetic
stages—embryonic fish, embryonic furry animals, finally
being born as larval primates.

In our early postnatal years we recapitulated this cycle once again. As amoeboid babies, floating and suck-
ing in our mothers' arms, we had neither the neurology
nor musculature to handle gravity. Then as crawling
infants we retraced the amphibian stage. As toddlers and
running cubs, we recapitulated the mammalian steps. As
parroting, mimicking children and as kids hanging out in
gangs, we relive the neolithic and hunter-gatherer stages
of our species past

Psychedelic Recapitulating

Experiential recapitulation of these genetic stages can be
found in the reports of almost every LSD tripper—the
experience of being a one-celled creature tenaciously
flailing, the singing, humming sound
of life exfoliating; you are the DNA
code spinning out multicellular esthetic solutions. You directly and
immediately experience invertebrate
joy—you feel your backbone forming;
gills form. You are a fish with glisten-
ing gills, the sound of ancient fetal
tides murmuring the rhythm of life.
You stretch and wriggle in mammalian
muscular strength, with loping, powerful, big muscles;
you sense hair growing on your body as you leave the
warm broth of water and take over the earth.

> Experiential
> recapitulation
> of the genetic
> stages is
> found in reports
> of LSD trippers.

The easiest interpretation is psychiatric: "Oh, everyone knows that LSD makes you crazy, and your
delusions can take any psychotic form. " But is it entirely
inconceivable that our cortical cells or the DNA molecules inside the cellular nucleus "remember" back along
the unbroken chain of bioelectrical transformations to
that original seeding in the Precambrian mud, for which
our language has few or no descriptive terms?

Recent breakthroughs in physics, genetics, and
neurologic are eliminating impersonal change and blind
accident from the philosophy of science and substitut-
ing intelligent choice. Physics, always highest, fastest,
quickest among the sciences, provides the gifts of relativity, singularity, multiple reality, mental choice,
quantum indeterminacy. Bohr's atom really is his own
idea. Now, after the Golden Age of Physics, comes the
Golden Age of Biology.

Gaia Theory

The Gaia theory, first presented by John Lovelock and
Lynn Margulls in 1978, defines one Life Organism with a
DNA brain and a spherical shape, which covers, surrounds, roots itself in the geosphere—the rocky planet.
This glorious conception suggests that a Life Intelligence
deftly, confidently, intelligently creates and maintains
the Biosphere, the film of slime which surrounds this
round rock in antiseptic—almost—space.

The Biosphere is an incredibly delicate, intricate,
cybernetic, ecological web in which evolution precisely
unfolds. Organisms equipped with nervous systems capable of attaining higher altitudes, velocities, and communication systems, eventually allow lifepods to blow
off the planet, like seed blossoms, and thus disseminate
Gaia around the galaxy.

Gaia's strategy is clear-cut and straightforward. First you land seed pods on a lifeless, rocky planet. Next create an atmosphere—air-ocean—in which life can infiltrate and surround the geosphere. The atmosphere fabricated by Gaia includes the ozone, the air, the oceans, the water cycle, and the topsoil—all results of biological processes. The Biosphere, the spherical film of life, then keeps temperature viably constant, and continually stirs up and co-mingles biotic and organic molecules from the crust elements, using wind currents and water movements as arteries.

Preprogrammed into Gaia's DNA brain are the codes for building more and more mobile organisms, which can perform all the above maintenance and dissemi-

> Gaia's strategy is clear-cut and straightforward.

nation functions more efficiently. Gaia evolves faster, stronger, and more intelligent forms, which eventually develop escape velocity sufficient to leave the planet. These seed-blossom space packets—of which the early, crude forms were Apollo, Soyuz, Skylab, Shuttle-Rocket—are structurally more intelligent and efficient because in a space capsule the geosphere surrounds and protects the inner Biosphere and atmosphere. Gaia thus constructs mini-worlds in which S/he moves us all around the galaxy.

Philosophized

In the 1960's, over seven million Americans took LSD and activated circuits in their brains that provoke heightened sensuality, understanding of the neural-nature of reality, and genetic, evolutionary ruminations. The first results were confusing—millions of instant philosophers babbling about God and love and bliss and

space and reincarnation. Now, twenty years later,
we are harvesting the fruits of this disorganized, mass
brain- scrambling.

The highest incidence of psychedelic drug use was in
the universities. Today re-
search centers and laboratories
are filled with scientists whose
brains were philosophized
while experimenting with LSD
in college and who are now
developing new methods,
new hypotheses, new theories
which are liberating humanity
from the dogmatic rule, superstitious religion, conservative,
pessimistic science. While cell
biologists have been learning
how Gaia moves personnel and
material around the planet, micro- geneticists and DNA
researchers have succeeded in deciphering the genetic
code. Recombinant engineering allows humans to create
new life forms, to correct malfunctioning genes, to
clone, to effect DNA repair, to understand and manage
the genetic signals which cause aging and death.

> Research centers
> and laboratories
> are filled with
> scientists whose
> brains were
> philosophized while
> experimenting
> with LSD in
> college.

Chapter 11

Ultimates

N uclear physicists and quantum theorists take as their subject matter the basic structure of matter/energy. Surely there is no form of worship as basic as this attempt to understand how things are made. One would think that the religious organizations, ministers, and publications would follow with bated breath the new revelations about the emission and absorption of energy by matter and the motion of elementary particles. One would hope that intelligent philosophers would continually be updating their theories in line with the new physical insights.

> *God #8 is the Quantum Physicist. The Eighth God is the creator of the universe and of the atom. The Eighth Craft of God is Quantum Mechanics.*

God the Quantum Physicist

Psychedelic subjects regularly report experiencing events that seem to harmonize with quantum mechanics. They speak of participating in and merging with pure— content-free—energy, white light; of witnessing the breakdown of macroscopic objects into vibratory Patterns, the

awareness that everything is a dance of particles, sensing
the smallness and fragility of our system, of world-ending
explosions, of the cyclical nature of creation and disso-
lution and so forth. I need not apologize for the flimsy
inadequacy of these words. If God were to let you whirl
for a second into the atomic nucleus or spin you out on a
light-year trip through the galaxies, how on earth would
you describe what you saw when you got back? Ask
someone who has taken a heavy dose of LSD.

It is of crucial philosophic importance to understand
that neurology, genetics, and quantum physics are all—in
their separate narrow vectors into the future—coming
to understand that evolving human
intelligence is apparently designed to
shape the universe, to navigate the
process of evolution, and to fabricate
the structure of personal reality. All
modern sciences accept and pay respect
to the subjectivity of the experimenter.

> Evolving human
> intelligence is
> apparently
> designed to
> shape the
> universe.

To understand that you are de-
signed to be God-the-Universe-Creator, you must first
grasp the implications of the Heisenberg principle of de-
terminacy—abjectly, cravenly, primitively called indeterminacy. Heisenberg's wonderful, liberating discovery
states that the scientist determines the nature of experiment. Modern quantum physics is currently producing
scenarios involving multiple realities, indeed, infinite
universes, determined by the attitudes and mental
structures and measurements of the observer. Prominent
and distinguished physicists have actually suggested that
the universe which we measure with our instruments is a
production of our thought.

Chapter 12

Tools of Experimental Theology

To master these Eight Divine Crafts may seem hopelessly Utopian. Actually, to ascend these levels of neurotechnology is becoming routine, because there now exist instruments to move intelligence to any desired level. The laboratory instruments for experimental theology, for internal science, are brain-activating chemicals—drugs, dope. Psychoactive drugs turn on the Eight Brain Circuits that mediate the levels of reality-experience:

The Origin Experience Is Possible

Anyone can noodle back down to swampy amoeboid, unicellular, vegetative beginnings by self-administering narcotics, ketamine, heavy doses of barbiturates. These neurochemicals turn off higher circuits of the brain and permit one to float in marine rapture. Three Quaaludes, for example, make it impossible to walk or master gravity.

Emotional Stupor

Mammalian Excitement can be attained by alcohol or
angel dust, which turn off the higher, cerebral centers and activate the midbrain. If you have mammalian
feelings of rage, dominance, power, which you wish to
experience—and to express in a safe- protective environment—these drugs will do it.

Mental Acceleration

Mental acceleration is produced by cocaine, pep pills,
and similar daily energizers—drugs that stimulate mental
performance, propelling you into busy game manipulations. Don't expect creativity, however.

Domesticated Virtue

Social security is produced by tranquilizers, including
the familiar Valiums, Libriums, Thorazines. Indeed, it
has been suggested that tranquilizers are the "glue" that
holds the American middle class together in dulled,
calm security.

   The warm, cozy, comfortable feeling that Everything
is Okay, that one is accepted and approved by the Hive
Society, can also be maintained by television, pop religion, movies. Heads of state feel tranquil when they see
the flag raised; the Iranian feels tranquil when he joins
thousands of others in cheering the Ayatollah. Catholics
feel the same wash of piety when they watch the pope
stride to his altar.

The Esthetic-Sensory-
Hedonic-Erotic Experience

The esthetic- sensory- hedonic- erotic experience is produced by any post- domestic psychedelic, mind- opening
drug. Low doses of LSD, mescaline, psilocybin, DMT

can turn off the 4 lower circuits—stupor, excitement, mental obsession, domestic virtue—and free the brain to experience direct- raw- naked- nerve- ending sensation. The traditional triggers for sensory awareness and chakra bliss are marijuana, hashish, and similar hedono- erotics.

The Ontological Revelation

The ontological revelation that the brain fabricates realities is produced by strong psychedelic—"mind- manifesting"—drugs, which allow one to observe the neuro-electric nature of consciousness. Drugs including LSD, mescaline, and psilocybin, give access to the billion- cell loom of flashing impulses and produce new imprints or new realities.

The Teleological-Evolutionary Experience

The teleological evolutionary experience can be produced by strong charges of psychedelic drugs. Psychedelic literature abounds in descriptions of pre- incarnation voyages down one's cellular pathways - two- way conversation between the central nervous system and RNA and DNA.

The Cosmological Experience

The neuro- astronomical revelation has been reported by many psychedelic experimenters. Many believe that the boom in space consciousness reflected in the movies *2001*, *Star Wars*, *Star Trek*, and such are predictable sequelae of the Neurological Revolution of the 1960's. Our knowledge as to which drug turns on which levels of consciousness is empirical, based on thousands of

psychedelic experiences. There is haunting phenomeno-
logical evidence that spiritual insights accompanying the
psychedelic experience might be subjective accounts of
the objective findings of astronomy, physics, biochemis-
try, and neurology.

Question Your Advisor

No matter how parsimonious our explanations, LSD
subjects do claim to experience revelations into the basic
questions, and do attribute life change to their visions.
How can you judge? Well, whenever you hear anyone
sounding off on internal freedom and consciousness- expanding foods and drugs—whether pro or con—ask these
questions.

Considerations in Evaluating Psychedelic Experts

Is your expert talking from direct experience, or
simply repeating cliches? Theologians and intellectuals often deprecate "experience" in favor of "moral
imperative. " Most often this classic debate becomes
a case of "experience" versus "inexperience. "

Do hir words spring from a philosophic- scientific
view? Is s/ he motivated by basic questions, or is
s/ he protecting hir own socialpsychological in-
vestment? Is s/ he riskily struggling toward all- out
sainthood, or maintaining a hive conformity?

How would hir argument sound if heard in an
African jungle hut, a ghat on the Ganges, in
Periclean Athens, in a Tibetan monastery, or in
a bull session led by any one of the great religious
leaders? Or on another planet inhabited by a su-
perior form of life? Or how would it sound to other

species of life—to dolphins, to the consciousness of a redwood? In other words, break out of your usual earphones and listen with the ears of another of Gaia's creatures.

How would the debate sound if you had a week to live, and were thus less committed to mundane issues? Our research group received many requests for consciousness- expanding experiences from terminal patients.

Does the point of view open up, or close down? Are you being urged to explore, experience, join a collaborative voyage of discovery? Or are you being pressured to close off, protect your gains, play it safe, accept the authority of someone who knows best?

Does your psychedelic expert use terms that are positive, pro- life, spiritual, inspiring, based on faith in your potential? Or does s/ he betray a mind obsessed by danger, material concern, ter- rors, administrative caution, or essential distrust in your potential? There is nothing in life to fear; no philosophic game can be lost.

If s/ he is against what s/ he calls "artificial methods of illumination, " ask hir what constitutes the natural. Words? Rituals? Tribal customs? Prime time TV?

If s/ he is against biochemical assistance, where does s/ he draw the line? Does s/ he use nicotine? Alcohol? Penicillin? Vitamins? Conventional sacramental substances?

If your advisor is against the neurotechnology of drugs, what is s/ he for? If s/ he forbids you the psychedelic key to revelation, what does s/ he offer instead?

Uncharted Territory

The Harvard Psychedelic Drug Research Project's first
goal was to train scientist- technicians in the use of powerful brain- change chemicals. LSD provided us with a
method of changing consciousness and brain function—
the tool that philosophers and psychologists had been
anticipating for centuries. Our problem was that there
was no scientific literature on the subject. The situation
was very similar to that of Janssen, Galileo, Malpighi,
Leeuwenhoek, early users of the microscope, which
dramatically expanded human perception, opening up
entirely new levels of reality. It was
obviously necessary to develop man-
uals to guide others in the use of the
new instrument.

> Like Janssen,
> Galileo, Malpighi,
> Leeuwenhoek, we
> had no scientific
> literature to
> bolster us.

Our first step was to plead en-
lightened ignorance. Any attempt
to label- limit the activated brain's
potentials was premature. Our sec-
ond step was to scan, sift, scour the libraries for books
on mystic experience. When all was read and said,
it seemed to us that the best "clinical, " step- by- step
description of a psychedelic experience yet published was
The Tibetan Book of the Dead. This classic Buddhist
text outlined the stages of the dying- rebirth process over
a period of 49 days. Though couched in primitive rural
language, the highs and lows, the "hallucinations" and
visions were clearly similar to the altered states our Harvard subjects experienced.

During the summer of 1962 I went through The
Tibetan Book of the Living—as we re- named it—line by
line, translating Buddhist imagery into American psychedelic jargon. The mimeographed versions were "tried
out" on hundreds of LSD trippers, and the polished,

revised version published by University Books in 1964.
Since that time, *The Psychedelic Experience* has been
reissued in nine hardback editions and several paperback
reprintings. Hundreds of thousands of LSD experiences
have been guided by this manual. Because of mass- mer-
chandising techniques, ironically, this book has probably
turned on more persons to the Gautama's teachings than
any single text since the Buddha's enlightenment 2, 500
years ago—although I doubt that you could get the Buddhist professional to admit it.

Chapter 13

Planning a Session

Having read this preparatory manual one can immediately recognize symptoms and experiences that might otherwise be terrifying, only because of lack of understanding. Recognition is the key word. Recognizing and locating the level of consciousness. This guidebook may also be used to avoid paranoid traps or to regain transcendence if it has been lost. If the experience starts with light, peace, mystic unity, understanding, and continues along this path, then there is no need to remember the manual or have it reread to you. Like a road map, consult it only when lost or when you wish to change course.

> Recognition key: Recognizing and locating the level of consciousness.

Set Goals

Classic Hinduism suggests four possible goals:

1. Increased personal power, intellectual understanding, sharpened insight into self and culture, improvement of life situation, accelerated learning, professional growth.

2. Duty, help of others, providing care, rehabilitation, rebirth for fellow men.

3. Fun, sensuous enjoyment, esthetic pleasure, interpersonal closeness, pure experience.

4. Transcendence, liberation from ego and space-time limits; attainment of mystical union.

The manual's primary emphasis on the last goal does not preclude other goals—in fact, it guarantees their attainment because illumination requires that the person be able to step out beyond problems of personality, role, and professional status. The initiate can decide beforehand to devote the psychedelic experience to any of the four goals.

In the extroverted transcendent experience, the self is ecstatically fused with external objects, such as flowers or other people. In the introverted state, the self is ecstatically fused with internal life processes—lights, energy waves, bodily events, biological forms. Either state may be negative rather than positive, depending on the voyager's set and setting.

For the extroverted mystic experience, one would bring to the session candles, pictures, books, incense, music, or recorded passages to guide the awareness in the desired direction. An introverted experience requires eliminating all stimulation—no light, no sound, no smell, no movement.

If several people are having a session together, they should at least be aware of each other's goals. Unexpected or undesired manipulations can easily "trap" the other voyagers into paranoid delusions.

Preparation

Psychedelic chemicals are not drugs in the usual sense of the word. There is no specific somatic

The better the preparation, the more ecstatic and revelatory the session.

or psychological reaction. The better the preparation, the more ecstatic and revelatory the session. In initial sessions with unprepared persons, set and setting—particularly the actions of others—are most important.

Long-range set refers to personal history, enduring personality, the kind of person you are. Your fears, desires, conflicts, guilts, secret passions, determine how you interpret and manage any psychedelic session.

Perhaps more important are the reflex mechanisms, defenses, protective maneuvers typically employed when dealing with anxiety. Flexibility, basic trust, philosophic faith, human openness, courage, interpersonal warmth, creativity, allow for fun and easy learning. Rigidity, desire to control, distrust, cynicism, narrowness, cowardice, coldness, make any new situation threatening.

Insight is the most important. Most important is insight. The person who has some understanding of hir own machinery, who can recognize when s/he is not functioning as s/he would wish, is better able to adapt to any challenge— even the sudden collapse of hir ego.

Immediate Set

Immediate set refers to expectations about the session itself. People naturally tend to impose personal and social perspectives on any new situation. For example, some ill-prepared subjects unconsciously impose a medical model on the experience. They look for symptoms, interpret each new sensation in terms of sickness/health, and, if anxiety develops, demand tranquilizers.

Occasionally, ill-planned sessions end with the subject demanding to see a doctor. Rebellion against con-

vention may motivate some people who take the drug.
The naive idea of doing something "far out" or vaguely
naughty can cloud the experience.

Turn Your Mind Off

LSD offers vast possibilities for accelerated learning and
scientific- scholarly research, but for initial sessions, intellectual reactions can become traps. "Turn your mind
off" is the best advice for novitiates. After you have
learned how to move your consciousness around—into
ego loss and back, at will—then intellectual exercises
can be incorporated into the psychedelic experience.
The objective is to free you from your verbal mind for as
long as possible.

Religious expectations invite the same advice. Again,
the subject in early sessions is best advised to float with the
stream, stay "up" as long as possible, and
postpone theological interpretations.

Recreational and esthetic expectations are natural. The psychedelic experience provides ecstatic moments that
dwarf any personal or cultural game.
Pure sensation can capture awareness.

> "Turn your mind off" is the best advice for novitiates.

Interpersonal intimacy reaches Himalayan heights. Esthetic delights—musical, artistic, botanical, natural—
are raised to the millionth power. But ego- game reactions—"I am having this ecstasy. How lucky I am! "—
can prevent the subject from reaching pure ego loss.

Scheduling

The subject should set aside at least three days—a day
before the experience, the session day, and a follow- up
day. This scheduling guarantees a reduction in external
pressure and a more sober commitment. Talking to oth-

ers who have taken the voyage is excellent preparation, although the hallucinatory quality of all descriptions should be recognized.

Allow time for reflection and meditation. The day after the session should be set aside to let the experience run its natural course and allow time for reflection and meditation. A too-hasty return to game involvements will blur the clarity and reduce the potential for learning. It is very useful for a group to stay together after the session and share and exchange experiences.

Observe a Session

Observing a session is another valuable preliminary. Reading books about mystical experience and of others' experiences is another possibility. Aldous Huxley, Alan Watts, and Gordon Wasson have written powerful accounts, for example.

Meditation

Meditation is probably the best preparation. Those who have spent time in the solitary attempt to manage the mind, to eliminate thought and reach higher stages of concentration, are the best candidates for a psychedelic session. When the ego loss occurs, they recognize the process as an eagerly awaited end.

Setting

First and most important, provide a setting removed from one's usual interpersonal games, and as free as possible from unforeseen distractions and intrusions. The voyager should make sure that s/he will not be disturbed; visitors or telephone calls will often jar hir into hallucinatory activity. Trust in the surroundings and privacy are necessary.

Time of Day

Many people are more comfortable in the evening, and consequently their experiences are deeper and richer. The person should choose the time of day that seems right. Later, s/ he may wish to experience the difference between night and day sessions. Similarly, gardens, beaches, forests, and open country have specific influences that one may or may not wish. The essential thing is to feel as comfortable as possible, whether in one's living room or under the night sky.

> The essential thing is to feel comfortable.

Familiar surroundings may help one feel confident in hallucinatory periods. If the session is held indoors, music, lighting, the availability of food and drink, should be considered beforehand. Most people report no hunger during the height of the experience, then later on prefer simple, ancient foods like bread, cheese, wine, and fresh fruit. The senses are wide open, and the taste and smell of a fresh orange are unforgettable.

Group Trips

In group sessions, people usually will not feel like walking or moving very much for long periods, and either beds or mattresses should be provided. One suggestion is to place the heads of the beds together to form a star pattern. Perhaps one may want to place a few beds together and keep one or two some distance apart for anyone who wishes to remain aside for some time. The availability of an extra room is desirable for someone who wishes to be in seclusion.

Chapter 14

The Psychedelic Guide

ith the cognitive mind suspended, the subject is in a heightened state of suggestibility. For initial sessions, the guide possesses enormous power to move consciousness with the slightest gesture or reaction.

The key here is the guide's ability to turn off hir own ego and social games, power needs, and fears—to be there, relaxed, solid, accepting, secure, to sense all and do nothing except let the subject know hir wise presence.

A psychedelic session lasts up to twelve hours and produces moments of intense, intense, INTENSE reactivity. The guide must never be bored, talkative, intellectualizing. S/he must remain calm during long periods of swirling mindlessness. S/he is the ground control, always there to receive messages and queries from high-flying aircraft, ready to help navigate their course and reach their destination.

> The guide does not impose hir own games on the voyager.

The guide does not impose hir own games on the voyager. Pilots who have their own flight plan—their own goals—are reassured to know that an expert is down there, available for help. But if ground control is harboring hir own motives, manipulating the plane towards selfish goals, the bond of security and confidence crumbles.

Ethics

To administer psychedelics without personal experience is unethical and dangerous. Our studies concluded that almost every negative LSD reaction has been caused by the guide's fear, which augmented the transient fear of the subject. When the guide acts to protect hirself, s/he communicates hir concern. If momentary discomfort or confusion happens, others present should not be sympathetic or show alarm but stay calm and restrain their "helping games." In particular, the "doctor" role should be avoided.

The guide must remain passively sensitive and intuitively relaxed for several hours—a difficult assignment for most Westerners. The most certain way to maintain a state of alert quietism, poised in ready flexibility, is for the guide to take a low dose of the psychedelic with the subject. Routine procedure is to have one trained person participating in the experience, and one staff member present without psychedelic aid. The knowledge that one experienced guide is "up" and keeping the subject company is of inestimable value—the security of a trained pilot flying at your wingtip; the scuba diver's security in the presence of an expert companion.

> The guide must remain passively sensitive and intuitively relaxed for several hours—a difficult assignment for most Westerners.

Experience Required

The less experienced subject will more likely impose hallucinations. The guide, likely to be in a state of mindless, blissful flow, is then pulled into the subject's hallucinatory field and may have difficulty orienting hir-self. There are no familiar fixed landmarks, no place to put your foot, no solid concept upon which to base your thinking. All is flux. Decisive action by the subject can structure the guide's flow if s/he has taken a heavy dose.

Rewarding New Profession

The psychedelic guide is literally a neurological liberator, who provides illumination, who frees men from their lifelong internal bondage. To be present at the moment of awakening, to share the ecstatic revelation when the voyager discovers the wonder and awe of the divine life-process, far outstrips earthly game ambitions. Awe and gratitude—rather than pride—are the rewards of this new profession.

Chapter 15

Ego Loss

S uccess implies very unusual preparation in consciousness expansion, as well as much calm, compassionate game playing—good karma—on the part of the participant. If the participant can see and grasp the idea of the empty mind as soon as the guide reveals it—that is to say, if s/he has the power to die consciously—and, at the supreme moment of quitting the ego, can recognize the ecstasy that will dawn upon hir and become one with it, then all bonds of illusion are broken asunder immediately. The dreamer is awakened into reality simultaneously with the mighty achievement of recognition.

It is best if the guru from whom the participant received guiding instructions is present. But if the guru cannot be present, then another experienced person, or a person the participant trusts, should be available to read this manual without imposing any of hir own games. Thereby the participant will be put in mind of what s/he had previously heard of the experience.

Illumination

Liberation is the nervous system devoid of mental-conceptual redundancy. The mind in its conditioned state,

limited to words and ego games, is continuously in
thought-formation activity. The nervous system in a
state of quiescence, alert, awake but not active, is com-
parable to what Buddhists call the highest state of *dhyana*
or deep meditation. The conscious recognition of the
Clear Light induces an ecstat-
ic condition of consciousness
such as saints and mystics of
the West have called illumination.

> The nervous system in
> a state of quiescence,
> alert, awake but not
> active, is comparable
> to what Buddhists call
> the highest state of
> *dhyana* or deep
> meditation.

The first sign is the
glimpsing of the "Clear Light
of Reality"—"the infalli-
ble mind of the pure mys-
tic state"—an awareness of
energy transformations with no imposition of mental
categories.

The duration of this state varies, depending on
the individual's experience, security, trust, preparation, and the surroundings. In those who have a little
practical experience of the tranquil state of non-game
awareness, this state can last from 30 minutes to several hours. Realization of what mystics call the "Ultimate Truth" is possible, provided that the person has
made sufficient preparation beforehand. Otherwise s/
he cannot benefit now, and must wander into lower and
lower conditions of hallucinations until s/he drops back
to routine reality.

Liberated State

It is important to remember that consciousness-expan-
sion is the reverse of the birth process, the ego-loss experience being a temporary ending of game life, a passing
from one state of consciousness into another. Just as an

infant must wake up and learn from experience the nature of this world, so a person must wake up in this new
brilliant world of consciousness expansion and become
familiar with its own peculiar conditions.

In those heavily dependent on ego games, who dread
giving up control, the illuminated state endures only for
a split second. In some, it lasts as long as the time taken
for eating a meal. If the subject is prepared to diagnose
the symptoms of ego-loss, s/he needs no outside help at
this point. The person about to give up hir ego should
be able to recognize the Clear Light. If the person fails
to recognize the onset of ego loss, s/he may complain of
strange bodily symptoms that show s/he has not reached
a liberated state.

Common Bodily Sensations

1. Bodily pressure
2. Clammy coldness followed by feverish heat
3. Body disintegrating or blown to atoms
4. Pressure on head and ears
5. Tingling in extremities
6. Feelings of body melting or flowing like wax
7. Nausea
8. Trembling or shaking, beginning in pelvic regions
   and spreading up torso.

Handling Physical Symptoms

The guide or friend should explain that the symptoms indicate the onset of ego- loss. These physical reactions are signs heralding transcendence—avoid treating them as symptoms of illness. The subject should hail stomach messages as a sign that consciousness is moving around in the body. Experience the sensa-

> Physical reactions are signs heralding transcendence.

tion fully, and let consciousness flow on to the next phase. It is usually more natural to let the subject's attention move from the stomach and concentrate on breathing and heartbeat. If this does not free hir from nausea, the guide should move the consciousness to external events—music, walking in the garden, etc. As a last resort, heave.

The physical symptoms of ego- loss, recognized and understood, should result in peaceful attainment of illumination. The simile of a needle balanced and set rolling on a thread is used by the lamas to elucidate this condition. So long as the needle retains its balance, it remains on the thread. Eventually, however, the pull of the ego or external stimulation affects it, and it falls.

In the realm of the Clear Light, similarly, a person in the ego- transcendent state momentarily enjoys a condition of perfect equilibrium and oneness. Unfamiliar with such an ecstatic non- ego state, the average consciousness lacks the power to function in it. Thoughts of personality, individualized being, dualism, prevent the realization of nirvana—the "blowing out of the flame" of fear or selfishness. When the voyager is clearly in a profound ego- transcendent ecstasy, the wise guide remains silent.

Chapter 16

Imprinting the
Taoist Experience

G n 1960-63, we Harvard drug researchers realized that we did not know enough about
the enormous range of reactions activated by
brain-change drugs. Even after hundreds of voyages aloft, our veteran test pilots reported amazing new
dimensions of galaxies within. For this reason we decided
to postpone any navigational mapmaking of our own.
Every week, new evidence changed the maps. We felt
like those 16th Century cartographers in Western Eu-
rope eagerly debriefing crews returning from the New
World. *The Tibetan Book of the Living,* our first venture
in updating old neurological-trip maps, was so successful
we became alarmed. Thousands of people began using
the Tibetan jargon of Bardos, and a definite fad-trend
towards Buddhism was developing.

To head off this prescientific Oriental renaissance,
we quickly sought another, less parochial text for describing and guiding brain astronauts. The advantage of
the *Tao Te Ching* was that this Taoist text was almost
content-free. There are no pious monks, shaved heads,
red hats, yellow hats, orange robes, or specific levels of
heaven, purgatory, and hell in the *Tao Te Ching.*

The *Tao* celebrates the constant flow of evolution, the eternal flow of always- changing energy process- es. The basic advice of Taoism—"Everything changes according to regular cycles and rhythms. So keep cool, watch the ebb and flow—and when the waves are ready, surf them. "

Tao Te Ching

The Chinese *Tao Te Ching*, sometimes translated as The Way of Life—written some 2, 600 years ago by one or several philosophers known to us now as "the old fel- low"—Lao- Tse—will remain timelessly modern as long as man has the same sort of nervous system and deals with the range of energies he now encounters.

Tao is best translated as "energy, " or energy pro- cess—energy in its pure unstructured state—the "E" of Einstein's equation—and in its countless, temporary states of structure—the "M" of Einstein's equa- tion. The *Tao* is an ode to nuclear physics, to life, to the genetic code, to that form of transient energy struc-

> The message of the *Tao Te Ching* is that all is energy, all energy flows, all things continually transform.

ture we call "man, " to those most static, lifeless forms of energy we call man's artifacts and symbols. The message of the *Tao Te Ching* is that all is energy, all energy flows; all things continually transform.

The *Tao Te Ching* is divided into 2 books—the first comprising 37 chapters, the second 44. It is a series of 81 verses that celebrate the flow of energy, its manifes- tations, and, on the practical side, the implications for man's endeavors. Most of the pragmatic sutras of the Tao were directed towards the ruler of a state and his ministers. Like all great texts, the Tao has been rewritten and reinterpreted in every century, the terms for Tao also change in each century. Advice given by philosophers to their emperor can be applied to how to run your home, your office, and how to conduct a psychedelic session.

Translation to Psychedelese

During that period I wrote *Psychedelic Prayers* from *Tao Te Ching*—the first book ever specifically designed to reimprint human brains during the "critical periods" of neural vulnerability. By the way, it is the second book explicitedly designed as a brainwashing manual. The insidious aim of this Dr. Frankenstein gambit was to prepare young people taking large doses of LSD to absorb a new reality- view based on post- Einsteinian, DNA science.

Psychedelic Prayers has probably bent over 200,000 young brains.

Over the years since thousands of young people with doctorates have entered careers in science, whose brains were directed by this book of hymns, odes, and paeans to the atom, to the DNA coil, and to the brain. *Psychedelic Prayers* has been reprinted over 20 times and has probably bent over 200,000 young brains.

These translations from English to psychedelese were made while sitting under a bamboo tree on a grassy slope of the Kumaon Hills overlooking the snow peaks of the Himalayas. I had 9 English translations of the Tao. I would select a Tao chapter and read and reread all 9 English versions of it. Each Western mind, of course, made his own interpretation of the flowing calligraphy. But after hours of rereading and meditation, the essence

of the poem would bubble up. Slowly a psychedelic version of the chapter would emerge.

The first-draft version would then be put under the
psychedelic microscope. For several years I pursued the
demanding yoga of one LSD session every seven days.
And each time our Moslem cook
walked down to the village, he would

For several
years I pursued
the demanding
yoga of one
LSD session
every seven
days.

bring back a crayon-size stick of attar,
"essence," of the resin of the marijuana plant sometimes called hashish.
LSD opened up the lenses of cellular
and molecular consciousness. Attar
cleansed the windows of the senses. During these sessions, I would
read the most recent draft of the *Tao*
poems. A humbling experience for the poet—to have hir
words exposed to pitiless psychedelic magnification.

Chapter 17

Psychedelic Prayers

Psychedelic poetry, like all psychedelic art, is crucially concerned with evolution, flow, change. Each psychedelic poem is carefully tailored for a certain time in the sequence of the session. Simplicity and diamond purity are important to the "turned on," intellectual flourishes and verbal pyrotechnics are painfully obvious. To the static intellect these sutras are simply another sequence of lifeless words. But to consciousness released from imprinted statics, these prayers can become precise bursts of trembling energy and breathless meaning.

Why Prayer?

You will wonder, perhaps, at the use of the term "prayer" to label these sutras. Prayer is ecstatic communication with your inner navigational computer. You cannot pray to an external power; that is begging. You cannot—without regret—communicate during the ecstatic moment in static prose.

When you are out beyond symbols, game communication seems pointless, irrelevant inappropriate, there is no need to communicate—because everything is already in communication. But there are those transition mo-

ments of terror, isolation, reverence, gratitude . . .
when there comes that need to communicate with the
energy source you sense in yourself and around you—at
the highest and best level you are capable of.

There is the need, at exactly that moment, for a
straight, pure, "right," non-game language. This is
prayer, mantra, lyrical harmony, verbal mathematics.
This need has been known and sensed for thousands of
years. All prayers are originally communications with
higher, freer energies—turning your-
self in to the energy dance.

Prayer is
ecstatic
communication
with your inner
navigational
computer.

Conventional prayers, for the
most part, have degenerated into parrot rituals, slogans, mimicked verbal-
izations, appeals for game help. But,
when the ecstatic cry is called for,
you must be ready to address Higher
Intelligence, to contact energy beyond
your game. You must be ready to pray. When you have
lost the need to address the Higher Intelligence, you are
a dead man in a world of dead symbols.

Each poem in this volume was exposed to several
dozen appraisals by lysergized nervous systems. A ruth-
less polishing and cutting away took place. The most
blatant redundancies and mentalisms were pruned. Most
psychedelic pilgrims found 5 or so poems in this collec-
tion which vibrate in tune to their deepest resonances.
The rest did not pass inspection.

Sheathing the Self

The play of energy endures
                    beyond striving
The play of energy endures
            beyond body
The play of energy endures
        beyond life

Out here float timeless
        beyond striving.

The Manifestation of the Mystery

Gazing, we do not see it
     we call it empty space.
Listening, we do not hear it
     we call it silence or noise.
Groping, we do not grasp it
     we call it intangible.
But here . . . we . . . spin through it
     electric, silent, subtle.

Please Do Not Clutch at the Gossamer Web

*All in Heaven and on Earth below
Is a crystal fabric. . . ...
Delicate gossamer web
Grabbing hands shatter it
Watch closely
this shimmering mosaic
Silent . . .
Glide in
Harmony*

The Serpent Coil
of DNA

We meet it everywhere
        but we do not see its front.
We follow it everywhere
    but we do not see its back.
When we embrace
    this ancient serpent coil
We are masters of the moment
    and feel no break in the
    curling back to primeval beginnings.
This may be called unravelling
    the clue of the life process.

The Seed Light

The seed light shines everywhere, left and right.

All forms derive life from it.

When the bodies are created, it does not take possession.

It clothes and feeds the ten thousand things

And does not disturb their illusions.

Magical helix smallest form and mother of all forms

The living are born, flourish and disappear

Without knowing their seed creator

Helix of light

In all nature it is true that the wiser, the oldest and the greatest resides in the smaller.

The Touch Chakra

Extend your free nerve
endings. . . trembling
Fine tendrils wove in skin
   feel my finger touch
   soft landing on your
   creviced surface
Send sense balloon drifting
   up through fifty miles of
Spindle-web skin tissue
   atmosphere electric thrill contact
   soar free through million
   mile blue epidermal space
   of cotton candy
Fragile web of nerve wire
   shuddering fleece of
   breathless pleasure.

The Sex Chakra

Rainbow
Can you float through
the universe of your body
and not lose your way?
Can you lie quietly engulfed in the
slippery union of male and female?
Warm wet dance of generation?
Endless ecstasies of couples?
Can you offer your stamen trembling in
the meadow for the electric
penetration of pollen while birds sing?
Writhe together on the river bank,
waft soft-feathered, quivering, in
the thicket?
Can you coil serpentine while birds sing?
Become two cells merging?
Slide together in molecule embrace?
Can you, murmuring, lose all...
fusing rainbow.

The Heart Chakra

Scarlet
Can you float . . . through
*   the universe of your body . . .*
*   and not lose your way . . .?*
Can you flow . . . with fire-blood
*   through each tissued corridor . . .?*
Throb . . .
*   to the pulse of life . . .?*
Can you let your heart . . .
*   pump you . . .*
*   down long red tunnels . . .?*
Radiate. . . swell . . . penetrate . . . to
*   the bumpy rhythm?*
Can you stream . . .
*   into cell chambers . . . ?*

Can you center . . .
　on this heart-fire of love . . .?
Can you let your heart . . .
　become central pump-house . . .
　for all human feelings?
Pulse for all love?
Beat for all sorrow?
Throb for all pain?
Thud for all joy?
Can you let it . . .
　beat for all mankind?
Burst . . . bleed out . . .
　into warm compassion
　flowing . . . flowing . . . pulsing . . .
　out . . . out . . . out?
Bleed to death
　life . . .
　blood
Scarlet

The Moment of Fullness

*G**rab hold tightly,
    let go lightly.
The full cup can take no
  more.
The candle burns down.
The taut bow must be loosed
    the razor edge cannot long
    endure.
Nor this moment re-lived.
So . . .
    now grab hold tightly.
Now . . .
    let go lightly.*

Chapter 18

You Are a God, Act Like One

Our Do-It-Yourself-God-Kit Program—the latest step in Self-Determination and the evolution of intelligence which was published in an East Village underground paper in 1966—is of considerable historic interest—not for what it says, but for what it does not say. Our self determining theology was rooted in the premise: Control your own brain, be your own Divinity, make your own world. Master the God Technologies. It pointedly did not repeat the injunction classically used by religious prophets—Follow me, sign up in my flock. It imposed no dogma except one—Live out your own highest vision.

> Our do-it-yourself religion did not demand: Follow me, sign up for my flock.

Turn On

The experienced psychedelic adept can move consciousness from one level to another. But then the experience must be communicated, harmonized with the greater flow. The "turned on" person realizes that S/he is not an isolated, separate social ego, but rather one transient energy process hooked up with the energy dance around hir.

Control your own brain, be your own Divinity.

The "turned on" person realizes that every action is a reflection of where S/he is at. The "turned on" person knows hir world is created by hir consciousness- existing only because S/he has arranged hir sensory and neural cameras to shoot these particular scenes. Hir movements, dress, grooming, room, house, the neighborhood in which S/he lives, are exact external replicas of hir state of consciousness. If the outside environment doesn't harmonize with hir state of mind, S/he knows that S/he must move gracefully to get in tune.

Tune In

"Tune in" means arrange your environment so that it reflects your state of consciousness, to harness your internal energy to the flow around you. If you understand this most practical, liberating message, you are free to live a life of beauty.

Let us consider a sad illumination. The Manhattan office worker moves through a clutter of factory- made, anonymous furniture to a plastic, impersonal kitchen, to breakfast on canned, packaged anonymous food- fuel; dresses hirself in the anonymous- city- dweller costume, travels through dark tunnels of sooty metal and gray concrete to a dark metal room, foul with polluted air. All day s/he deals with symbols that have no relevance to his divine possibilities. This person is surrounded by the dreary, impersonal, assembly- line, mass- produced, anonymous environ-

Live out your own highest vision.

ment of an automated robot, which perfectly mirrors hir "turned off" awareness.

When this person "turns on," S/he sees at once the horror of hir surroundings. If S/he "tunes in," S/he begins to change hir movements and hir surroundings so that they become more in harmony with hir internal beauty. If everyone in Manhattan were to "turn on" and "tune in," grass would grow on First Avenue and tieless, shoeless divinities would dance or roller-skate down the car-less streets. Ecological consciousness would emerge within 25 years. Fish would swim in a clear-blue Hudson.

> Every action of a human being reflects hir state of consciousness.
>
> Every person is an artist who communicates hir experience.

Every action of a human being reflects hir state of consciousness. Therefore, every person is an artist who communicates hir experience. Most people are not "tuned in" consciously. They experience only in terms of static, tired symbols. Therefore, their actions and their surroundings are dead, robot art.

Drop Out

After you "turn on," you must "tune in": start changing your dress, your home, to reflect the grandeur and glory of your vision. But this process must be harmonious and graceful. No abrupt, destructive, rebellious actions, please start "tuning in" through your body movements. Walk, talk, eat, drink like a joyous forest-dwelling god.

Next change your dwelling place. If you have to live in the city for the time being, arrange your apartment so that it becomes a shrine. Your room should reflect a timeless, eternal beauty. Every object should make immediate sense to the sense organs of a visitor from the 6th Century B. C. to the 21st Century A. D.

When you have made your body a sacred temple and

Your State of Consciousness is Reflected in Your Environment

your apartment a navigational, seduction cabin in a 21ˢᵗ Century time-ship you are ready to change your broader social commitments. Do not "drop out" until you have "tuned in. " Do not "turn on" unless you know how to "tune in, " or you will get "hung up! " Every "bad trip" is caused by the failure to "tune in. " Here's why. …

What Happens

When you "tune in" you open up neural receptors. Cannabis flicks on sensory receptors, hashish somatic receptors, LSD cellular and molecular receptors. These forceful energies cannot be harnessed to a hive-ego game board. You cannot hook up 100 million years of sensory-somatic revelation to your puny, trivial-personality chessboard. You cannot access 2 billion years of evolutionary revelation to your petty social program. This is why marijuana and LSD, if used in a closed system, will, sooner or later, freak you out.

Of over 5, 000 persons who have begun the yoga of LSD with me, the large majority could not harness their activated energies to a more harmonious game. You cannot take LSD once a week and stay rigidly rooted in a low-level ego game. You have to grow with the flow, or you will stop taking LSD. To continue to use LSD, you must generate around you an ever-widening ring of "tuned in" actions. You must hook up your inner power to a life of expanding intelligence.

How to Tune In & Drop Out

1. Go home and look at yourself in the mirror. Start changing your dress, your behavior, so that you float like a god, not shuffle like a robot.

2. Look around your home. What kind of dead robot lives here? Start throwing out everything that is not "tuned in" to your highest vision.

3. Make your body a temple, your home a shrine.

4. You are a God, live like one!

Grow
with
the
flow.

Chapter 19

LSD as a
Sacrament

9 n September 1966, working with First Amendment lawyers, we formally founded a new religion, called the League for Spiritual Development, to provide legal protection for our own neurological investigations and to encourage others to form their
own religions. We made very clear that the league was
not a mass organization but was limited to 100 people
centered around the Millbrook estate in Dutchess Coun-
ty, New York. We were not seeking to convert, but to
show others how to do it themselves.

Our first sacramental assembling, a religious celebration at the Village Theatre in New York's Lower
East Side, was based on the "Magic Theatre" sequence
from Hermann Hesse's *Steppenwolf*. It was a bead- game
multimedia performance deliberately designed to "blow
minds," to overload nervous systems with ever- changing
Niagaras of moving forms, some familiar, some nov-
el. The sound track blasted with acid rock, Oriental
chants, synthesizer whirls, body noises, heartbeats,
heavy breathings—all highly amplified. A video orches-
tra of 9 performers manipulating slide projectors play-

ing over double- and triple- exposed films. Psychedelic
prayers and a spoken narrative guided viewers through
the reenactment of Harry Haller's mystical trip.

A Sensation

The Psychedelic Celebrations were a sensation. Enormous worldwide publicity, sold- out
performances. I was nominated for
best Off- Broadway actor of the year.
Hollywood film people thronged to
the events.

> We inspired the
> horrid Hindu
> Paisley-print
> boom.

The Hesse drama was followed
by a celebration of The Attempted
Assassination and Escape of Jesus Christ, which parodied
the Catholic Mass. Then, A Life of the Buddha. The
50 light- soundstage artists who produced these events
were the originators of what became Psychedelic Art,
2001 Hollywood special effects, dance- hall light shows.
We were also guilty of inspiring the horrid Hindu pais-
ley- print boom.

When television commercials took over our tech-
niques, we knew it was time to quit. "Turn on to
Squirt. Tune in to Taste. Drop Out of the Cola rut!"
We did.

Wild Generalizations

I was quoted in a Playboy interview, saying that if you
take LSD in a nuthouse, you will have a nuthouse experience. Later a Village Voice journalist generalized with
the question: If a student were to take LSD in this rat
race environment, would he have a rat race experience?

The reporter was asking for a wild generalization.
No one should take LSD unless s/ he's well prepared,

knows what s/he's getting into, is ready to go out of hir mind. Hir session should be in a place that will facilitate a positive, serene reaction, with someone s/he trusts emotionally and spiritually.

Contrary to what many suppose, I never gave drugs to any minors—including any undergraduate at Harvard. We did give psychedelic drugs to many graduate students, young professors, and researchers who were well trained and prepared for the experience. They were doing it for a serious purpose; to learn more about consciousness, the game of mastering this technique for their own personal life and professional work.

> The aim of taking LSD is to develop yourself philosophically, increase your intelligence, open up greater sensitivity. After the session, therefore, the exciting process you have begun should continue.

LSD Psychosis

Many people fear recurrences of the LSD psychosis without further ingestion of the drug. I can't agree with the word "psychosis." The aim of taking LSD is to develop yourself philosophically, increase your intelligence, open up greater sensitivity. After the session, therefore, the exciting process you have begun should continue. We're delighted when people tell us that after their LSD sessions they can flash back to some of the illumination, meaning, and beauty. We know that we are producing philosophic experiences, and we and our subjects aim to have those experiences endure.

If nobody knows exactly what LSD does—and I share that worry—we must realize that scientifically we are not sure of the effects of gas fumes, DDT, penicillin, tranquilizers on the individual and the genetic structure of the species. There are risks involved. Nobody should take LSD unless s/ he knows s/ he's going into the unknown, laying hir blue chips on the line. But you're taking a risk every time you breathe the air, every time you eat the food the supermarkets are putting out—every time you fall in love. Life is a series of risks, for that matter. We insist

> If you listen to neurologists and psychiatrists, you'd never fall in love.

only that the person who goes into it knows it's a risk, knows what's involved. No paternalistic profession like medicine has the right to prevent us from meeting that challenge. If you listen to neurologists and psychiatrists, you'd never fall in love.

Flashbacks

There are going to be recurrent memories and reactions, when you hear the same music, are with the same people, walk into the same room. Any stimulation may set off a memory—a live, chemical molecular event in your nervous system.

When you take LSD, you're changing that system to a small degree. Most people are delighted when this happens. But when a professional full-time worrier takes LSD, s/ he's going to wonder if s/ he's going crazy, if s/ he's insane, s/ he's going to worry about brain damage, about germs, loss of precious body fluids. Worriers, of course, want everything under control. But life is spontaneous, undisciplined, unsupervised. Your worrier is going to lay hir worrying machinery on LSD. The psychedelic experience can be philosophic if the person is looking for it, and even if the person is not looking for it. People use different interpretations, different metaphors to describe their religious experience. A Christian will take LSD and report it in terms of the Christian vocabulary. CIA agents will look for communists.

Akin to Hinduism

Our philosophy about the meaning of LSD comes closer
to Hinduism than to any other religion. Hinduism is a
pagan philosophy that recognizes the divinity of all man-
ifestations of life, allowing for a wide scope of sub-sects.

> I was influenced
> by Hermann
> Hesse's
> Siddhartha,
> very much so.

To a Hindu, Catholicism is a form
of Hinduism.

As many have noted, descriptions of the psychedelic experience
sound very much like Hermann
Hesse's *Siddhartha*. I was influenced
by his writings—very much so.

Of course, in philosophic and literary interpretations
of consciousness expansion, most great writers basically
agree on the necessity of going out of your mind, going
within, and about what you find once you get there.
Metaphors change from culture to culture, but every
great mystic and visionary reports the same eternal flow,
timeless series of evolutions, and so forth.

Our first psychedelic celebration in New York ad-
dressed the intellectual trapped in hir mind. For that
first celebration we were using *Steppenwolf* as our "bible. "
The next psychedelic celebration was based on the life of
Christ, and for that we used the Catholic missal as the
manual. After that, we ran celebrations of Socrates,
Einstein, Gurdjieff.

Each celebration was intended to take up one of the
great religious or philosophic traditions. Our purpose was
to turn on everyone to that religion. We hoped anyone
that came to all our celebrations would discover that
each of these great myths is based on a psychedelic experience, a death-rebirth sequence. But in addition, we
hoped that the Christian would be particularly turned on

by our Catholic LSD Mass, because it renewed the resurrection metaphor, which for many has become rather routine and tired. The aim was to turn on not just the mind, but the sense organs, and even to talk to people's cells and ancient centers of wisdom.

After You Turn On

I was ovulated, fertilized, and born in the 20th century. I can't wipe out my whole personal background, or the fact that almost everyone I talk to today is brain-damaged by our education. I think American education makes us hopeless symbol addicts. It's designed to produce docile automatons. But it's going to take 15 to 20 years before you can urge young people to drop out of school without appearing to be an eccentric or a madman.

> Almost everyone today is brain-damaged by our education, which is designed to produce docile automatons.

There are three processes involved that every spiritual teacher has passed on to humanity for the past thousand years. First, look within, glory in the revelation. Second, then express it in acts of glorification on the outside, and third, detach yourself from the current tribe.

After you turn on, don't spend the rest of your life contemplating the inner wonders. Begin immediately expressing your revelation in acts of beauty. That's very much a part of our religion—the glorification, the acting out, the expression of what you have learned. That's what we were doing in the Village Theatre. Every Tuesday night people came there, and we stoned them out of their minds—all without LSD.

To do anything new, you have to change your nervous system. You can do it through breathing, fasting, flagellation, dancing, solitude, diet; you can do it through any sense organ- visual, auditory, and so forth. There are hundreds of ways of turning on. But at present, very few people can use these methods, so drugs are almost the only specific way an American is ever going to have a religious experience.

Our Tuesday night celebrations did not take the place of the sacrament. In our religion the sacramental process is the use of marijuana and LSD; and nothing can substitute for that.

LSD for Kicks

When I'm accused of promoting the use of LSD for kicks, I wonder what they mean by "kicks. " To me, the kick means an ecstatic revelation. To you, a kick may mean going to a cocktail party and flirting with some girl. A kick to me means a pagan flirtation with God—Gaia. Of course, in our Puritan society, we think we should work, get power, and use this power to control other people. In any sane society, the word kick could be the ideal, the ecstasy. It means going beyond, getting out of your mind, confronting God.

> A kick to me means a pagan flirtation with God—Gaia.

A confrontation with divinity, your own higher intelligence, is going to change you, and some people don't want to change. They should be warned that if you come into this temple, you're going to face blazing activation of your brain. You're never going to be the same. In the Eleusinian mysteries, they would always warn people, "if you go in here, your ego will die. You're going to have to confront all your past hang- ups,

strip them off, and be a changed person. " One emperor
of Rome who wanted to be initiated in the Eleusinian
mysteries said, "That's interesting, I approve of what
you're doing, but I don't want to be changed. " Everyone is somewhat afraid to take LSD, because everyone
wants to keep hir own little egocentric chess game going.

Fear of LSD

There's everything to fear. You're going to go out of
your mind. But if LSD really worked the way the fear
merchants say it does, it would be easy to take the crim-
inal and the alcoholic, the drug addict, and the generally mean person and change them under guidance. But
our conditioned mental processes are highly resistant to
change. If you take LSD, you still come back speaking
English and knowing how to tie your shoelaces.

The problem is that you do step back into routine
ways of thinking. That's why if you take LSD, you
should plan to slowly change your environment, harmonize your external commitments
with internal achievements. It's
very hard work to change the
human psychology. That should
comfort the frightened and challenge the fast-lane, quick-change
optimist like myself.

> If you take LSD,
> you still come back
> knowing how to tie
> your shoelaces.

The trip as well as the contemplation of it afterwards
are equally important. One without the other is rather
meaningless. After a session, we may go plant a new
garden, change a room in the house, or throw out the
frozen-canned foods. I may spend the next five hours
talking quietly with my son.

Law of Jiu-Jitsu

I don't use the term "harassment"; the game I am involved in is like the Harvard-Yale game. Harvard isn't
harassing Yale. The game between the establishment
and the utopian visionaries will inevitably exist in every
historical era. It's fair that they want to hound me out of
existence, just like the Harvard defensive team wants to
throw the Yale quarterback for a loss. I have no com-
plaint about this.

> Law of Jiu-Jitsu:
> The more energy that is
> directed against me, the more
> energy is available for me.

The more en-
ergy that is directed
against me, the more
energy is available
for me- it's the law of
jiu-jitsu. To us, the
government and professional-establishment dynamism
against what we were doing was just a sign that we were
doing fine.

Chapter 20

A Holy Mess

R esearch on the interpersonal reflex in 1957
demonstrated how humans fabricate and
maintain their own personal worlds. By 1966
this self-responsibility message was expanded
from the interpersonal to the neurological realm. Your
actions determined the environment you inhabited.
Divinity was within, and the word "God"
was understood to refer to the Higher Intel-   Only the
ligence resident within one's own brain and   young
within one's own DNA. The aim was to   listened.
provide a socially acceptable reason for tam-
pering with your own brain and increasing intelligence.

As the 1960's exfoliated, the religious metaphor
continued to boomed. To our dismay. Jesus Christ,
what a holy mess! We told people that they were gods—
only the young listened. And we published two books
and scores of essays and interviews pushing The Journey
to the Eastern Lobes of the Brain.

It worked because it was so seductive. There
was a lot to learn back-East—the barefoot grace,
the body-control sinuosity of yoga, the wiry elastic
mind-trick of seeing everything from the standpoint of

eternity. The ultimate cool of fatalism. The junky- hindu grin of pompous, self- satisfied passivity. The comforting babble of mantra nonsense- syllables. New, colorful, bizarre Hindu Lord's Prayers to monkey- mimic.

Most cults and religions that sprang up in the 1960's and 1970's recruited docile "followers. " The Mansons, the Moons, the Jim Joneses, the swamis, the Born- Again Preachers all play on the prim- itive, prescientific, infantile loser desire to submit to a parental authority figure. The crisp advice transmitted in our do- it- yourself theology is—take responsibility for making your own life beautiful.

> Take responsibility for making your own life beautiful.

Wise Trickster

Oriental religions, like their Western counterparts, are elaborate rationalizations for avoiding change. The Eastern religious philosophies are the final flowering of the great pre- scientific wisdom that took us from the caves and taught us everything beautiful and harmonious that could be produced by a hand- tool culture. What- ever could be done with the body, including the vocal chords, had been developed and poetized by 100 genera- tions of Hindu- Buddhist adepts.

Oriental philosophy is profoundly pessimistic, cyni- cal, stoic, and passive. Before modern scientific tech- nology expanded the scope of human perception there was, indeed, no place to go and nothing new. The same old body cycle—circles of birth, aging, and death. Stay detached from the outer world, because there is nothing you can do about the relentless leveling entropy of age.

The Oriental posture is unbearably smug and certain. Nothing makes any difference, so cool out. It's all one, and it's all lost.

Gifts from the Magi

I took the obligatory trip to the East, scanned the guru scene, got the picture. The best Indian gurus are wise tricksters who have mastered the one simple rule of entropy—it's all going to hell, so get yourself a comfortable spot here and now, and let the fools who are still searching come and project their illusions—and their money— on your calm, cool, blank facade.

India is a sad country, run by bureaucrats. The British Civil Service mentality, patched onto the ultimate fussy pedantry of Brahminism, left everyone in a mean, petty mood. The Hindu antagonism towards change, scientific method, any active solution to problems, was depressing. It became clear that for 2,500 years, the most intelligent, energetic, attractive Indians had been migrating westward. India is not a place for fun-lovers, hope fiends, enthusiastic pro-lifers. But India still had a lot to teach us Westerners, and we returned from Benares loaded with paradoxical gifts from the Magi. We joyfully accepted and employed Oriental pagan techniques to pursue, more effectively, future Western goals.

We accepted the basic anti-Christian Hindu notion that the aim of this life is continual self-development, self-mastery, self-sufficiency. One could become a "perfect master," not of others, but of one's own body and brain. We used

We translated the basic Hindu teaching that everything is illusion into the modern neurological truth that everything is a figment of your own brain.

this insight in our image. We translated the basic Hindu teaching that everything is illusion into the modern neurological truth that everything is a figment of your own brain. We resolved to fabricate the illusion that, through science, we can decipher and discover—which really means create—new levels of energy, new layered realities, new stages of evolution.

Basic Paganism

We bought the Vedic notion of reincarnation—updated by modern genetics and expanded into the future. Neo-Lamarckianism is back in town in the guise of genetic engineering. True, everything we do in this lifetime fabricates our next incarnations, but these future realities can be created in our lifetime. Listen, I'll tell you about multiple reincarnations. I have sailed full-throttle through the Roaring 20's, the Boring 30's, the Booming 40's, the Consuming 50's, the Celestial 60's, the Terrestrial 70's. And all this has taught

> The good old basic paganism got everybody moving again.

me how to pre-incarnate for the Grateful-Fateful 80's and the Well-Designed 90's.

Everything we did in the 1960's was designed to fission, to weaken faith in and conformity to the 1950's social order. Our precise surgical target was the Judeo-Christian power monolith, which has imposed a guilty, inhibited, grim, anti-body, anti-life repression on Western civilization.

Our assignment was to topple this prudish, judgmental civilization. And it worked. For the first time in 20 centuries, the good old basic paganism got everybody moving again. White people actually started to move their hips, let the Marine crewcuts grow long, adorn themselves erotically in Dionysian revels, tune into nature.

The ancient Celtic-pagan spirit began to sweep through the land of Eisenhower and J. Edgar Hoover. Membership in organized churches began to plummet. Hedonism, always the movement of individuals managing their own rewards and pleasures, ran rampant.

Millions of Americans exulted in the old Celtic Singularity. Every woman a queen, every man a king; God within. The classic paganism now combined with the American virtues of do-it-yourself, distrust of authority. Millions of Americans writing their own Declarations of Independence—my life, my liberty, my pursuit of happiness.

Millions of marijuana smokers, adepts in hatha yoga, and meditators experienced the neural level of consciousness—transcended symbols and contacted raw energy hitting their nerve endings. At least another million LSD, peyote, and mushroom eaters, contacted cellular consciousness—have had experiences transcending both symbolic game and sensory apparatus. Next we have those who have taken large doses of LSD, mescaline, DMT, and have contacted the molecular and elemental energies within the cellular structure, experiencing the "white light," the "void," the "inner light."

If we add those millions of institutionalized mystics who have had involuntary psychedelic experiences, this group swells to astounding proportions. Each of these different psychedelic levels—neural, cellular, molecular—is beyond symbols, incoherent to the symbolic mind. Most psychedelic voyagers are aware of the limitless realities in the nervous systems, but there is no conception of the meaning and use of these potentials.

Alas, most of these explorers couldn't handle the freedom or independence. The familiar hunger for authority, the recurring obsession to submit; to give responsibility to a master. George Harrison grovels in front of the Maharish. Poor Bob Dylan submits to Christ. Peter Townshend babbles inanities about Meher Baba.

Swarms of gurus and spiritual-teachers run around announcing new commandments, new prohibitions.

> The word "religion" translates "to bind" from the Latin.

The word "religion" beautifully defines itself, of course. It translates "to bind" from the Latin—"re" means back and "ligare" means to tie up. All religions are straitjackets, jackets for the straight. Look at the faces of the followers—the Hare Krishnas, for example—and you'll get the point. Pimpled losers who don't like their own looks and have no love of their own singularity.

Jackets for the Straight

We learned a lot. We were disappointed that for every new-breed, self-confident scientist popping up on the scene, there were 99 new cult-followers. There was a gloomy period when I felt bewildered guilt at having encouraged this lemming-like rush to Eastern bonds.

The master-follower thing was particularly annoying. I despise followers of any kind, especially those who follow me. As it happens I am not alone in this distaste; no one really likes followers. Followers do not like them-

selves, of course; that's why they crawl. And masters
have nothing but contempt for their subservants, which
is why they impose such colorful embarrassments upon
them.

Religious Freedom

I despise
followers of
any kind,
especially
those who
follow me.

But a glance at American history was
comforting. Since the Pilgrims, the
Quakers, the Mormons, the Emersonian
Transcendentalists, our frontier country
has always seethed with kooky cults and
splinter messiahs. The amazing Indepen-
dent religiosity, the off-the-wall fervor of
Americans has always been a wonderful
source of eccentric individuality.

There were, after all, no Jehovah's Witnesses or
Hare Krishnas running around Franco's Spain or the
Soviet Union. I was also comforted by the thought that
the new religiosity was part of our wonderful aristocratic
American consumerism, the Insatiable American tel-
evoid brain demanding new sensations, new surprises,
new heroes, new reality scripts.

You are a God

Act like one!

—Timothy Leary

Grow
with
the
Flow!
—Timothy Leary

Printed in the USA
CPSIA information can be obtained
at www.ICGtesting.com
JSHW082221140824
68134JS00015B/667

9 781579 510527